The Peasants' Revolting: Lives

For all the men and women, like Wat Tyler, who struggled to make a difference. Their names are mostly lost, but their efforts mustn't be forgotten.
At least they tried. We owe them.

The Peasants' Revolting: Lives

Stories of the worst of times
lived by the underclasses
of Britain

Terry Deary

PEN & SWORD HISTORY

First published in Great Britain in 2020 by
Pen & Sword History
An imprint of
Pen & Sword Books Ltd
Yorkshire – Philadelphia

ISBN 978 1 52674 561 3

Printed and bound in the UK by
CPI Group (UK) Ltd, Croydon, CR0 4YY.

Pen & Sword Books Limited incorporates the imprints of Atlas, Archaeology,
Aviation, Discovery, Family History, Fiction, History, Maritime, Military, Military
Classics, Politics, Select, Transport, True Crime, Air World, Frontline Publishing,
Leo Cooper, Remember When, Seaforth Publishing, The Praetorian Press,
Wharncliffe Local History, Wharncliffe Transport, Wharncliffe True Crime and
White Owl.

For a complete list of Pen & Sword titles please contact

PEN & SWORD BOOKS LIMITED
47 Church Street, Barnsley, South Yorkshire, S70 2AS, England
E-mail: enquiries@pen-and-sword.co.uk
Website: www.pen-and-sword.co.uk

Or

PEN AND SWORD BOOKS
1950 Lawrence Rd, Havertown, PA 19083, USA
E-mail: Uspen-and-sword@casematepublishers.com
Website: www.penandswordbooks.com

Contents

Contents

Introduction

The past is a foreign country: they do things differently there.

L.P. Hartley (1895–1972), British novelist

Historians are often asked by their readers, 'If you could live at any time in history, which would you choose?'

The person asking the question probably has a favourite era of their own, seen through the golden-tinted spectacles of school history books – the ones with colourful pictures.

⇨ Tudors? Ruffs to hide your wrinkled neck and a carriage to take you to see Mr Shakespeare's latest blockbuster.
⇨ Georgians? All those wigs and colourful fashions. What's not to like?
⇨ The Victorians? The thrill of the steam trains and an expanding empire to explore.

The sensible historian will point out that almost any era could be pleasant for the top percentile of the population. For peasants (like you or me) the world would be a dirty and dangerous place, cruel and unfair with foul food and terrible toilets.

The sensible answer to 'Which era in history would you choose to live in?' would be 'THIS era. The NOW.'

After all, nothing is as far away as one minute ago.

Some historians have argued that there *has* been a 'Golden Age' ... the age of Elizabeth I is a popular choice. Yes, that glorious age when:

⇨ Catholics were tortured in The Tower before being hanged, drawn and quartered
⇨ when a Yorkshire housewife was pressed to death for hiding a priest
⇨ when a Scottish queen was beheaded very messily by a butchering executioner
⇨ when the Armada was defied by Britain's gallant sailors ... sailors who were left, unpaid, to starve on the streets.

Introduction

Yes, THAT golden age.

Where does this fantasy of a shining age come from? From those chroniclers of old who recorded the doings of the great.

Time, like an ever-rolling stream, bears all its sons away;
They fly forgotten as a dream dies at the opening day.
Isaac Watts (1674–1748), English minister and hymn writer

The 'forgotten' people of history are the peasants. They don't seem to count.

History is written not to revere the dead, but to inspire the living.
Simon Scharma (b. 1945), English historian

Are these clever historians – the ones who ignore the peasants – suggesting we can only be 'inspired' by the rich, the aristocrats and the leaders? Bookshops and libraries are packed with tomes about them.

The poor, the ignored and the forgotten, struggle to squeeze onto the shelves. Yet some of those peasants did something the 'great' and the good would have failed to do if their roles had been reversed. They survived.

You and I might not last a week in the world of a peasant. A week without our takeaways, our underfloor heating, our antibiotics … and, of course, our smartphones.

Just for a change, and just for a while, consider the life of the peasant rather than the life of a king or a conqueror.

You may be inspired by the courage and fortitude of our fellow humans.

And, when someone asks you, 'Which era in history would you choose to live in?' you might just answer with one word.

Now.

Chapter 1

Work

There is nothing laudable in work for work's sake.

John Stuart Mill (1806–1873), British economist

And John Stuart Mill has a point. Most people don't work for work's sake. They work to provide food, shelter and widescreen televisions for themselves and their family. And, even if you do have a compulsion to work for work's sake, it isn't a golden path to satisfaction and fulfilment.

I put my heart and my soul into my work and have lost my mind in the process.

Vincent Van Gogh (1853–1890), Dutch Post-Impressionist painter

Vincent ought to know. He produced about 2,100 artworks, including around 860 oil paintings, and sold precisely one in his lifetime. He 'lost his mind' and killed himself at the age of 37.

Peasants rarely had the chance to work for anything other than to keep their heads above the poverty line. Serfdom – like capital punishment – has been left in the peasant past, yet poverty remains.

Labour Party leader Tony Blair vowed in 1999 to eradicate child poverty completely by 2020. It's become a political football and surveys and statistics can't be trusted. But anecdotes are grim.

In April 2018, head teachers said children come into school malnourished and hungry. A head teacher said that after a school holiday – when the children have missed free school meals …

My children have grey skin, poor teeth, poor hair; they are thinner.

Another head said …

Monday morning is the worst. There are a number of families that we target that we know are going to be coming into school hungry. By the time it's 9.30 am, they are tired.

A Cardiff head teacher said …

Children often bring just a slice of bread and margarine for lunch.

By 2019, a report said that the number of children living in absolute poverty increased by 200,000 in 2017–18. As a result, 30 per cent of children, or 4.1 million, were living in relative poverty in the UK.

The politicians, like the lords of old, lament the miserable suffering of the underclasses and go home to find some small consolation in a fine feast.

To make the money to survive you could beg, borrow or steal. You could sell something … and most people sell their labour. They work.[1]

> *To live is to suffer, to survive is to find some meaning in the suffering.*
> Friedrich Nietzsche (1844–1900), German philosopher[2]

It may be a little tricky to find any 'meaning' in the suffering of the peasants through the ages.

The agricultural labourer

> *It is the custom in England, as with other countries, for the nobility to have great power over the common people, who are serfs. This means that they are bound by law and custom to plough the field of their masters, harvest the corn, gather it into barns, and thresh and winnow the grain; they must also mow and carry home the hay, cut and collect wood, and perform all manner of tasks of this kind.*
> Jean Froissart (1337–1405), French historian (written 1395)

A ploughman's lot is not a happy one.

> *His coat of a cloth that is thin as the East wind,*
> *His hood full of holes with his hair sticking through,*
> *His clumsy shoes, knobbled and nailed over thickly,*
> *Yet his toes poked clean through as he trod on the ground.*

---

1. Though that same 2019 Child Poverty report pointed out that 70 per cent of children living in poverty were in working families.
2. Friedrich Nietzsche famously said, 'God is dead. God remains dead. And we have killed him.' But by 1900, Friedrich Nietzsche was dead. God must have had a chuckle at that, don't you think?

Two miserable mittens made out of old rags,
The fingers worn out and the filth caked on them,
He waded in mud almost up to his ankles,
In front are four oxen, so weary and feeble
Their ribs could be counted, so wretched they were.

William Langland (1332–1386),
presumed author of *Piers Ploughman*

If Langland wrote the poem, and if he died around 1386, then he'd have lived through the bubonic plague and known of the 1381 Peasants' Revolt. It may sound as though Langland was sympathetic to the poor peasant. But when the peasants grumbled, he shrugged and said …

When hunger was their master none complained.

In other words, the peasants were getting too comfortable and too well fed. A good dose of famine would put them back in their place.

Overcoming poverty is not a gesture of charity. It is an act of justice.
Nelson Mandela (1918–2013), South African statesman,
speech in Trafalgar Square, London

Nelson Mandela, a rebel against racial injustice, would have had sympathy with the peasants who revolted against social injustice in 1381. Their brief reign of terror, remembered as the Peasants' Revolt, was a violent one and – unlike Mandela – they didn't significantly alter the status quo.[3]

Peasants revolting

Jampton: England is in danger. I tell you sir, thirteen men claiming to be the English nation are approaching here on foot.
Prime Minister: Oh? And whose foot are they approaching on?

From *The Goon Show*, December 1957,
script by Spike Milligan and Larry Stephens

The peasants may have revolted in 1381, but it was a minority of the population … just enough to make the history books. It helped that they

---

3. 'Status quo' – a fine phrase. I would never use Latin phrases simply to impress people. Oh no. It's just my modus operandi.

murdered a few top people along the way; otherwise the history books would have been a lot less keen to chronicle the events.

Why did they revolt, you ask? Glad you asked. I reply that it was like a chocolate advert from 1866 that said there were five stages to satisfaction. In the ad, a boy's five facial expressions ranged through …

⇨ *Desperation* – no chocolate
⇨ *Pacification* – the promise of chocolate
⇨ *Expectation* – the prospect of chocolate
⇨ *Acclamation* – happiness at receiving chocolate, and
⇨ *Realisation* – eating the chocolate and discovering that it is a Fry's milk chocolate bar.

Maybe the Peasants' Revolt followed that pattern but without the high calorie outcome?

1. Desperation

> *There is just so much hurt, disappointment, and oppression one can take. The line between reason and madness grows thinner.*
>
> Rosa Parks (1913–2005), American rights activist

Disaffected people revolt. But by 1381, it was not just disaffection … it was disappointment.

The peasants who had survived the Black Death believed they were *special* – God's chosen ones. And that gave them a new confidence. The peasants had seen a light at the end of the ploughman's furrow and the landowners tried to snuff it like a church candle.

The rebel souls may not have been able to read the Bible, but there were literate priests like John Ball from Kent who could quote and translate from the Latin …

> *If God be for us, who can be against us?*
>
> King James Bible, Romans 8:31

The peasants became swollen with self-importance like a helium-filled balloon … but without the laughs. Their argument was simple: 'We surviving peasants are worth more pay. That's according to the law of supply and demand.'

And if the landowners had spluttered 'The law of supply and demand hasn't been invented yet', the peasants would quote Ahmad Ibn Taymiyyah, the controversial mediaeval Sunni Muslim theologian, who said …

If desire for goods increases while its availability decreases, its price rises. On the other hand, if availability of the good increases and the desire for it decreases, the price comes down.

Ibn Taymiyyah (1263–1328), Sunni Muslim theologian and reformer

But the landowners – including the Church – had an answer to that. They introduced the Statute of Labourers in 1351. Its primary aim was to stop peasants profiting from the shortage of labour after the Black Death. Wages were limited to 2 pence a day. Many peasants were compelled to work, without pay, on Church land.

This Church obligation was tiresome as the peasants' time could have been used to work on their own land. However, the power of the Church was so great that few dared to break this rule. The workers had been taught from a very early age that God would see their sins and punish them in the next life.

They also had to pay a tax to the Church called a tithe – a tax of 10 per cent of the value of what a family had farmed of the farm produce. That 10 per cent could be the difference between feast and famine for the family.

What is the difference between a taxidermist and a tax collector? The taxidermist takes only your skin.

Mark Twain (1835–1910), American writer

As well as labour, a peasant could pay in cash or in kind (grain, animals or vegetables). The lords and Church sometimes demanded all three forms of payment – days of labour, a share of their produce and cash. The peasants – or villeins – never became inured to being under the well-heeled heels of the lords. In 1293, a Worcestershire man was told he must take on land owned by the Earl of Gloucester. That would reduce the man to villeinage. In desperation he threw himself into the river Severn and drowned.

The tithes kept the peasants on the cusp of starvation and, just to rub in the fact the Church was making a fortune, the bishops stored their ill-gotten goodies in huge tithe barns. Imagine if you were a hungry peasant walking on your way to your frozen field and having to walk past that barn stuffed with the bishop's food.

Some of these barns, like Tithe Barn in Maidstone, are preserved as scheduled monuments. Monuments? Monuments to the oppression of the peasants?

My attitude is, a monument ought to signify unity instead of division.
Bill Nelson (b. 1942), American politician

The leader of the Peasants' Revolt, Wat Tyler, released his priestly pal, John Ball, from Maidstone jail during the Peasants' Revolt in 1381. So that Maidstone Tithe Barn must have been a silent witness to the explosive rage of the peasants.[4]

These tithes and their monstrous barns may explain why the peasants targeted the clergy when they rose. When the revolting peasants overran the Tower of London, they found Archbishop Sudbury in the chapel of the White Tower. He was taken out to Tower Hill and beheaded. His head was paraded around the city, before being affixed to a pole over London Bridge.

Of course, when it came to collecting your tax, God had a lot of help from William the Conqueror's Domesday Book. The monarch on earth, and the one in Heaven, both knew how much you owed. The wages of sin may be death, but after they take the taxes out, it's more like a dose of the flu, really.

Frustration and *desperation* led to the Peasants' Revolt.

It's not the despair. I can take the despair. It's the hope I can't stand.
John Cleese, as Brian Stimpson in the film *Clockwise* (1986)

2. Pacification

What do we want?
A cure for dyslexia.
When do we want it?
Own

In the Middle Ages in Europe, the peasants had a short life, but a miserable one. The Black Death had reinforced the feeling that life was too short to

---

4. In some monasteries in the 1400s it's been revealed that monks were five times more likely to die of obesity-related joint diseases than the average peasant. Monks were eating wheat-bread. Peasants in 1437–40 were trying to survive on bread made from peas or even fern roots. Jolly, fat Friar Tuck of legend was a reality.

wait for your fortunes to take a turn for the better. Things were getting worse, if anything, so direct action was needed.

If the overwork didn't kill you then you could die from ordinary things like a rotten tooth.

Peasants certainly resented the two days a week when they worked for the Church, but carried on for the one, big benefit they would gain: a free pass into Heaven when they died. Jam tomorrow. Pacification.

Then a rumour went around that the Church did little to suppress. It said that a peasants' soul *didn't* get to Heaven – demons would refuse to carry it away. Why? Because of the horrible smell.[5]

With the expectation of Heaven fading like a mirage, the impatience for comfort NOW became more urgent.

> *History does not eliminate grievances. It lays them down like landmines.*
> A.N. Wilson (b. 1950), English writer, in *The Victorians*

The peasants of Britain squirmed under the yoke of their lords but were generally passive. What they needed was a good example of civil disobedience. It came from France.

3. Expectation

> *Life is so constructed, that the event does not, cannot, will not, match the expectation.*
> Charlotte Brontë (1816–1855), British novelist

And as far as 'expectation' goes, Charlotte Brontë must have been disappointed to have died at the age of 38. She can't have expected that.

The Peasants' Revolt began in May 1381, famously prompted by the levying of a poll tax of 4 pence per adult – peasant or aristo; you all paid the same.

Girls were exempt if they were virgins – leading John Legge, serjeant at law, to carry out public examinations. (This is a tax avoidance check no longer practised by HMRC.)

But where did the peasants get the 'expectation' that they could overthrow the feudal system? After all, the system was a pyramid and it's hard to sit

---

5. Who'd have thought demons could be so fussy? I've stood next to a few strap-hangers on the London Underground who would never get to Heaven … or even Hell.

at the bottom and tip it over. They were encouraged by the example from across the English Channel.

> *It may be we shall rise the last as Frenchmen rose the first*
> G.K. Chesterton (1874–1936), English writer, in *The Secret People*[6]

The French peasants of the 1300s were just as oppressed as their British counterparts and just as envious of the unattainable high life.

While the French peasants froze in the fields, died in ditches or starved in slums, the rich people had 'fun'. In the fourteenth century, Count Robert of Artois had a very pleasant garden. It had:

⇨ statues that squirted water at you as you walked past
⇨ a trapdoor that dropped you onto a feather bed
⇨ a hosepipe that squirted water up ladies' dresses
⇨ a statue that squawked at you like a parrot[7]
⇨ a room that greeted you with a thunderstorm as you opened the door.

No wonder the peasants hated the nobles in their castles. The peasants didn't go to school, but they could do basic arithmetic and they knew 'There are more of US than there are of THEM'.

In France, in 1358, they decided to test their mettle against their oppressors. This 1358 French rebellion was known as the Jacquerie. Maybe because any peasant was known as a 'Jacques' (a 'John', in English), so it was a revolt of the 'Johns'.

Maybe you prefer the explanation that it was because they wore padded, boiled-leather jackets as a sort of cheap armour and these jackets were called 'Jacques' – so it was a revolt of the padded-boiled-leather-jackets (which sounds much more poetic, don't you think?).

---

6. Chesterton predicted Brexit in this 1907 poem including the lines …
'They have given us into the hand of new unhappy lords,
Lords without anger or honour, who dare not carry their swords.
But we are the people of England; and we have not spoken yet.
Smile at us, pay us, pass us. But do not quite forget.'
7. What wouldn't we give for a mechanical parrot that squawks 'Who's a pretty garcon?' or 'Polly wants escargots'?

I am the son of peasants and I know what is happening in the villages. That is why I wanted to take revenge, and I regret nothing.

Gavrilo Princip (1894–1919), revolutionary[8]

These peasants weren't used to organising themselves, but the nobles were so remote from the underclasses they were slow to realise that rebellion was brewing like French vino de plonk.

⇨ At first, the Jacquerie murdered a few surprised nobles. The peasant leader was Guillaume 'Will' Cale, a relatively well-off farmer from the Beauvais region.
⇨ The Beauvais region had been hit by the Black Death but scarcely touched by the Hundred Years War with the English. It stayed prosperous … until the English captured their King John II and demanded a huge ransom. Taxes were raised to pay for his release and the Beauvais peasants suddenly felt aggrieved.
⇨ Armed with axes, scythes and pitchforks, a 10,000-strong army captured over a hundred castles. Knights fled with their families – or stayed and died.

> *Peasants killed a knight, put him on a spit, and roasted him with his wife and children looking on. After ten or twelve of them raped the lady, they wished to force-feed them the roasted flesh of their father and husband and made them die by a miserable death.*
>
> Jen le Bel (1290–1370), French chronicler

⇨ Charles of Navarre led the fightback and Charles used one weapon that Will Cale didn't have … the ability to lie convincingly. The peasants had numbers, the knights had cunning. They cheated. Charles suggested that they should talk and Cale, the clot, arrived to parley without a guard.[9]
⇨ Naturally, Navarre nabbed him and locked him in chains. His knights rode down Cale's supporters. Some chronicles say Cale was tortured to death by being crowned with a red-hot crown. He was certainly beheaded – with or without a crown.

---

8. Gavrilo only fired two bullets. He hit Austrian Archduke Ferdinand and Duchess Sophia. The assassination was the spark that exploded into the First World War. Gavrilo's two bullets killed 15 million people.
9. The knights behaved nobly and would never invite another knight to parley and then capture him. But Cale wasn't a knight. Rules of chivalry didn't apply to the underclasses. A loophole that Charles exploited … and Will Cale didn't even know existed.

⇨ Then there were reprisals against the Jacquerie. 'Peasant houses, fields and families will be destroyed,' the noble Navarre promised. Unlike his 'safe-passage' promise to Cale, the destruction was one promise Navarre kept. Knights roamed the country, lynching peasants for sport.

⇨ Around 150 noble victims were avenged by the deaths of an estimated 20,000 anonymous peasants.

The English peasants learned from their French cousins that peasants could revolt. But their historians forgot to tell them that a peasants' revolt could end very messily, that the word of a lord was not worth a cathedral candle. They didn't know – but should have guessed – that rebellion attracted reprisal.

4. Acclamation

I am not afraid of an army of lions led by a sheep; I am afraid of an army of sheep led by a lion.

Alexander the Great (356–323 BC), King of Macedon

The peasants were not sheep. They were not stupid. They didn't have 'schooling' like the lordly classes, and they weren't trained in 'leadership'. But there were charismatic men and women who emerged as natural leaders in times of crisis. Two who strode to the front of the 1381 Peasants' Revolt were Wat Tyler and John Ball.

We don't know much about people like Wat Tyler because his followers couldn't write his history ... and his enemies weren't interested in his origins. But he must have been a compelling individual. A lion leading a ragged army of lion cubs.

Who were these acclaimed leaders? Guesses say ...

⇨ Tyler/tiler was probably his occupation, not his family name.[10]

⇨ He lived in Dartford (Kent) ... or Maidstone or Deptford. (If there's no monument to the great man it's because no one knows who owns him.)

⇨ If Wat was the man of action then John Ball, a radical priest, was the philosopher. Ball was chronicled (by his enemies) as 'the mad priest of Kent' (Froissart). But since he wasn't 'of Kent', we can challenge the

---

10. Imagine a roofer having dreams of being a leader? A Tiler, or a Thatcher. It'll never happen.

'mad' epithet too. (Historians like Froissart can distort the truth to suit their purposes.)
⇨ Ball preached that all humans should be treated equally, as descendants of Adam and Eve.

> *When Adam delved and Eve span*
> *Who was then the gentleman?*
> *From the beginning all men by nature were created alike, and our bondage or servitude came in by the unjust oppression of naughty men. For if God would have had any bondmen from the beginning, he would have appointed who should be bond, and who free. And therefore, I exhort you to consider that now the time is come, appointed to us by God, in which ye may (if ye will) cast off the yoke of bondage, and recover liberty.*
>
> John Ball (1338–1381), English Lollard priest

⇨ He took to speaking to parishioners in churchyards after the church services. He spoke in English, the 'common tongue', not the Latin of the priests inside the church. John Ball threatened the status quo.
⇨ This fighting talk brought him into conflict with Simon of Sudbury, Archbishop of Canterbury. Ball was thrown in jail many times. He was released from Maidstone jail at the start of the Peasants' Revolt and that could be the beginning of his partnership with Tyler, who was from Maidstone … maybe.

Tyler and Ball – men worthy of peasant acclamation. To the Crown and Church establishment they were seen simply as a threat. They had to be stopped, then crushed.

5. Realisation

> REALISATION: noun. The making real of something imagined or planned.
> Dictionary

But reality doesn't always go as imagined or planned. Reality can bite.

Tyler's peasants marched on London to see the king. They murdered a few unpopular lords on the way and stuck their heads on long poles.

The numbers and the enthusiasm for rebellion were declining as peasants discovered the delights of the capital's hostelries. You can't loot and booze and protest all at the same time. It's a familiar story …

I'll shoot the aristocracy and confiscate their brass,
Create a fine democracy that's truly working class.
As soon as this pub closes, as soon as this pub closes,
As soon as this pub closes, I'll raise the banner high.

Alex Glasgow (1935–2001), English singer/songwriter

Wat's 20,000 rebels reached London and presented their demands …

⇨ no more poll tax
⇨ no more slavery for peasants
⇨ freedom to use the forests
⇨ freedom to hunt wild animals.

Like the Jacquerie, the English rebels were promised safe-conduct to parley. And, like their French antecedents, they were betrayed.

The story of his demise is well known. When Tyler went to meet young King Richard II, an argument broke out between Tyler and some of the royal servants. The Mayor of London, William Walworth, ordered Tyler to be arrested. Wat tried to evade arrest and that was Walworth's excuse to stab Tyler.

The Lord Mayor feared he'd harm the king, that was his true belief
And there at Smithfield drew his sword, and cut our captain down
And the heart went out of all of us with his blood upon the ground

Lyrics of *Wat Tyler*, sung by Fairport Convention

The 14-year-old King Richard II looked on, the man who had promised his subjects a peaceful resolution. As Richard II might have said …

Instead of a man of peace and love, I have become a man of violence and revenge.

Hiawatha (1525–1575), colonial American Indian leader

When the rebels had been sent back to their homes, Ball was taken prisoner, then hanged, drawn and quartered at St Albans in the presence of King Richard II. His head was stuck on a pike on London Bridge, just as Archbishop Sudbury's had been … in fact, Sudbury's dead head would have been removed to make way for his enemy's. He must have enjoyed that. The quarters of Ball's body were displayed at four different towns. There was to be no forgiving and forgetting.

To take revenge half-heartedly is to court disaster; either condemn or crown your hatred.

Pierre Corneille (1606–1684), French dramatist

And all because Wat Tyler hadn't read his history books. He hadn't learned from what had happened to Will Cale twenty-three years before.

But home to Kent like beaten dogs, still serfs we had to crawl

Wat Tyler song

We only learn from history if we are taught history.

Revenge is sweet … and not fattening.

Alfred Hitchcock (1899–1980),
English film director

Other rebellions sprang up and fell down. The world of the peasant family changed down the centuries; it didn't improve.

Working just to pay taxes was soul-destroying. Peasants through time had to become accustomed to working till they dropped, even if they were children.

Children growing up to work alongside their parents was a custom as old as time. But the Industrial Revolution brought children onto the market as employees. They were as cheap and expendable as a disposable lighter and eventually the world woke up to the horrors.

Child labour

They began work at 5.30 and quit at 7 at night. Children 6 years old going home to lie on a straw pallet until time to resume work the next morning. I have seen the hair torn out of their heads by the machinery, their scalps torn off, and yet not a single tear was shed, while the poodle dogs were loved and caressed and carried to the seashore.

Mary G. Harris Jones (1837–1930), known as Mother Jones,
schoolteacher/activist (commenting in the 1860s)

Peasant children had helped their parents in their survival as soon as they were able. There was no child-minding available (or needed) and the peasant child picked up the necessary skills to use in their own adult lives.

The Industrial Revolution, from the mid-1700s, changed that. Children were now cheap labour to employers and out of the hair and the purses of parents. Pauper children were often sold to masters as it meant their parents had one fewer month to feed – cash in hand and fewer future outgoings. Win-win.

Sweeps

Life is life. Some of the wisest people you meet are sweeping our streets.
Jeremy Corbyn (b. 1949), British politician

And if Mr Corbyn had lived 200 years ago, he may have added, 'and sweeping our chimneys'. Life – as he so sagaciously informs us – is indeed life. How true.

Basil Fawlty: Can't we get you on Mastermind, *Sybyl? Next contestant: Sybil Fawlty from Torquay, specialist subject – 'The Bleeding Obvious'.*
TV series *Fawlty Towers* (1975–1979),
writers Connie Booth and John Cleese

Some of the wisest people you meet are not politicians. Some of the dumbest people you meet are.

Talking of sweeping, sweeping chimneys was one of the jobs that was better done by children.

Once chimneys became *de rigueur* in the homes of the rich (from the 1500s onwards) there arose the need for chimney sweeps. All year round, coal was needed for heating water and cooking. The build-up of soot could easily catch fire and brushes on poles were not very efficient.

There WERE alternatives but it depends on how averse you are to animal cruelty. For centuries, geese were used in addition to children for chimney cleaning. The sweep tied the legs of the goose together and tossed it down the chimney. The flapping wings of the bird would knock the soot down, cleaning the chimney in the process.

The method was so normal it became a byword for the idea that it's good to get dirty.

The blacker the goose, the cleaner the flue.

Poor goose, you say? Maybe you'd prefer a skinny child? Then you are in luck because the average height of the population fell in the 1830s as the Industrial Evolution generation reached maturity with knock knees, humpbacks and twisted pelvises from standing fourteen hours a day.

The boy or girl sweeps climbed the narrow flues with a hand brush and scraper. Their hands, feet, knees and elbows were scraped raw, and the soot caused skin diseases and cancer.

Did you know ...?

It is considered good luck for one to see a chimney sweep on your wedding day. Shake hands with, or be kissed by one, is double the luck.[11]

To keep children small enough to climb the flues, they were poorly fed. And of course, it didn't pay to be too kind.

They were in their boyhood; the youngest six, the next seven and the third told me he was 'past nine a little bit and going on for ten'. They were all brothers and apprenticed to a huge, grim being, who damned the elder apprentice for leaving one of his brushes, with which he struck him on the shoulders and throwing, at the same time, two large pieces of dark bread into the darker hands of his two younger. The smallest was led by the master by the delicate, sable arm, shaking him at every step and bidding him to leave off whimpering, and not squeaking like a mouse, but cry his 'Sweep, sweep' like a man.

Quote from *Pratt's cleanings in England* (c. 1800)

The boy whined that he was tired and needed a rest. The master explained that chimneys had to be swept early, before the house-owners rose from their feathered beds and wanted a warm room to breakfast in ...

I have two chimneys to sweep now before half-past-eight in Covent Garden, and don't you hear St Martin's is now striking seven. There is one of the chimneys as crooked as a corkscrew that none but a shrimp as you can climb up.

Nice that he had a pet name – like 'Shrimp' – for his little charges. The master threw the boy over his shoulder, like a sack, and went into the

---

11. And if your marriage has been less than lucky, you now know where you went wrong. Life is a lottery ... or a sweep-stake.

house. The oldest of the boys told the chronicler that he would rather be a shoeblack or a galley slave than work for the master who starved and beat them. He went on …

> *I have nothing to sleep on but some of these sacks in a soot cellar. What's worse, my master won't allow us to wash, not once a month, so that I am quite sore with the clogged stuff that has almost eat into my flesh.*
>
> Quote from *Pratt's cleanings in England*

Clearly the word 'gratitude' was not in this child's vocabulary when it came to describe the home comforts he enjoyed.

If you were a sweep-master, you wouldn't want to pamper and spoil the brats, would you?[12]

Did you know …?

You can no longer push a cherub up a chimney. In 1842, Parliament passed a law banning the practice – but this did not stop sweeps using their own children to do work. Some used their offspring as young as 4 or 5 years old to go up chimneys. Finally, in 1864, an Act of Parliament outlawed the use of children for climbing chimneys, with a penalty of £10 for offenders.

Top tip: If your child-sweep is too slow – or is stuck up a chimney – light a fire in the hearth to encourage them. They may fall and die or suffocate, but the local workhouse will have some replacement.

Miners

> *I would much prefer to be a judge than a coal miner because of the absence of falling coal.*
>
> Peter Cook (1937–1995), British writer

Coal made the soot and the coal was mined with the help of children. So, they were at both ends of the process of keeping the rich folk warm. It's hard to say which end was the worse – the sweeping or the mining.

---

12. If you ARE planning on becoming a sweep-master then you can buy a child from an orphanage or – cheapest of all – pick up a homeless child off the streets. Don't thank me for the advice – just give me a discount on my chimney sweeping.

Work

1. An 1842 report said:

   Pit managers say they take children to work in the pits from the age of 9. Unfortunately, there is proof that children go down into many of the pits at a much earlier age. In some cases, as early as between 5 and 6.

   The pit managers blamed the parents who pestered them to take young children as workers.

2. Whatever the age, the work was hard. The report went on:

   In some pits the boys do not start work until 5 am and there are some pits where it is 6 am. But whatever time they start they have to work for twelve hours. In talking with the miners and boys I never found one of them complain of the early hour at which they went to work.

   Most wouldn't dare complain, of course. They worked – or they starved.

3. The work wasn't hard – children didn't dig and load the coal at the face – but it was miserable.

   His place of work is inside one of the doors called a trap-door. This door must be opened whenever men or boys, with or without carriages, wish to pass through. He seats himself in a little hole, about the size of a common fireplace, and with the string in his hand; and all his work is to pull his string when he must open the door, and when man or boy has passed through, then allow the door to shut of itself …
   He sits alone with no one to talk to him; for in the pit the whole of the people are as busy as if they were in a sea-fight … he himself has no light. His hours … are passed in total darkness.

4. And in the darkness there are other uncomfortable things:

   That the air of the pit does not destroy all life. Horses thrive well, and so do asses, if the pit be not too warm. Midges are in millions. Wood-lice are common, so are insects called forty-legs; and beetles are found in all parts of the pit.

   There's a nice bit of company as you sit in the dark.

5. If luck was water then Edward Morrow didn't have enough to fill a thimble. He was a trapper boy at the time when any trapper boy who failed to open a door on time would be whipped by the miners. Many fell asleep and woke up to a thrashing. Some fell asleep across the underground railway line. If a truck came along, they could lose a leg or lose their life. Edward Morrow was 7 years old when he first worked in a mine. On his first day he fell asleep and a truck sliced off his leg. James was fitted with a wooden leg and returned to his job three months later. (Some children lost their heads in truck accidents and a prosthetic wooden head was not an option.) Before he was nine, unlucky James was killed when a roof collapsed on him.

6. Many young trappers like Edward were killed when they fell asleep and slumped into the path of the carts. But there were other dangers too. Joseph Arkley was 10 when he forgot to shut a trapdoor.[13] That allowed poisonous gas to seep into the tunnel. He died along with ten others when the gas exploded.

7. Until 1842, women worked underground, as did children as young as 8. Victoria's inspectors put an end to that following a disaster at Huskar Colliery, near Barnsley, in which twenty-six children were killed. The inquiry resulted in the Mines and Collieries Act, banning women and girls, and boys under 10, from underground work.

8. Ban women and children? Oh, we wise people of the twenty-first century cry, how humane. Except not all Victorian reformers saw it that way. They weren't worried about the effect of the work on the *women*. They were worried about the effect on the *men*. The effect on their morality … and their mortal souls. Unbelievable, but true. An inspector wrote …

> *The chain used to pull the carts passes high up between the legs of two girls and had worn large holes in their trousers. Any sight more disgustingly indecent or revolting can scarcely be imagined. No brothel can beat it.*

Victorian prudishness. No other age can beat it.

And it was the rich who were celebrated for making Britain the wealthiest nation in the world. It was the rich who had statues erected to themselves. Statues that still stand.

One of the finest Victorian erections is in Durham City …

---

13. Ten years old was the *average* age of a child labourer during the 1830s. In practice, some were as young as 4.

How the other half lived

Charles William Stewart (1778–1854), Lord Londonderry, started his adult life as a soldier. His nickname was 'Fighting Charlie' for his army adventures around Europe. But he married the wealthy Lady Frances Anne Vane-Tempest and returned to look after her Durham coalfields … and her money.

All of the miners of Northumberland, Cumberland and Durham were employed under the hated Bond system. They were under contract and their labour was owned by the 'masters' like Londonderry. In 1839/40, for example, sixty-six pitmen in the county of Durham were jailed for short periods as 'vagrants'; their crime was to leave their usual places of work while 'bonded'.

In an 1844 strike, the miners demanded a living wage. Londonderry responded with the ruthless 'Seaham Letter', in which he warned all traders not to give credit to the strikers, or else they would become 'marked' men and would be put out of business.

His Lordship evicted any miner tenants involved in the strike and brought in replacements from his estates in the north of Ireland to act as strike-breakers. More evictions followed to make way for them. In 1822, the workers were earning a few pounds a year for a life of dirty and dangerous work. In that year, Lord Londonderry's Penshaw and Rainton collieries earned him £61,364.[14]

He brought income to Durham City and was rewarded with a statue that stands in the city's market square.

The men, women and children of the Durham coalfield did the work and suffered in the misery of the mines. What a shame there isn't room for a memorial to any of them.

Terrible textiles

Humility and knowledge in poor clothes excel pride and ignorance in costly attire.

William Penn (1644–1718), English writer

In the first half of the 1800s, the upper classes wore silks and cottons, they had glass jugs and steel knives on their tables, coal in their fireplaces and food

---

14. Lest you think the Londonderry family were heartless monsters, remember the Irish Famine. Lady Londonderry contributed to famine relief on her Irish estates. She gave £30.

on their plates. Almost all of it was produced by children working in terrible conditions just a stone's-throw away from the great houses. In that same era, the same upper classes wailed, gnashed teeth and campaigned against the slave trade while British children were regularly shackled and starved.[15]

Waterloo was (and is) celebrated as a triumph, but demobbed soldiers returned home to no country fit for heroes … and no pension. Young Thomas Sanderson went out to work as a child in the factories when his soldier-father returned destitute and the family was reduced to eating acorns that they had foraged. Others were so hungry that they were reduced to eating rats.

The peasant class, as ever, was peopled by the invisible.

> *The machine … is not dead.*
> *It reaches out a claw to clutch the hearts of men.*
> *Against the villages roll marching hosts,*
> *The fields are withered by their sulphurous breath,*
> *And stony wastes are left where children die,*
> *And men are governed by a cruel clock,*
> *That beats a doleful time,*
> *One shall be arm, another leg, a third brain,*
> *And the soul, the soul is dead.*
>
> Ernst Toller (1893–1939), German playwright,
> in *The Machine Wreckers*

Cotton made Britain a world power in trade. But when the fluffy stuff first arrived, the peasants of Britain were ignorant of where it came from. It looks like wool? Then it must come from sheep, but sheep that grow on trees.

> *There grew in India a wonderful tree which bore tiny lambs on the endes of its branches. These branches were so pliable that they bent down to allow the lambs to feed when they are hungry.*
>
> John Mandeville, travel writer (writing in 1530)

When enclosure had taken away the peasant families' ability to make a living from the land, they turned to cottage industries. Weaving and stocking-making were profitable – if unhealthy – ways of surviving.

---

15. Literally. Some children were shackled with ankle-irons riveted on and chains linked to their hips. This prevented them from escaping their work in the dark, satanic mills. They worked and slept in their chains.

Elizabeth I could have taken the credit (if she had lived long enough) for seeing the industry of stocking-weaving thrive. Legend has it that in 1561, she was presented with a pair of knitted, black stockings and would wear nothing else. A machine to weave stockings was invented. A story is told of how it came about …

Once upon a time, there was a student at Oxford who fell in love with the local innkeeper's daughter. The student – by marrying – lost his place at the college.[16] The penniless couple scraped a living from her one great skill … knitting stockings. The young man being a student, and so not fit for any form of manual labour, spent the idle hours watching his young wife work. He watched as the needles flew and her fingers too. Now, the young man may have been as useless as a brush to a bald-headed man when it came to labour, but he had a bit of a brain. He imagined a machine that would do the work of his wife … only faster. Thus was the stocking loom invented. Not only did the inventor place himself above poverty but he helped thousands of poor families to do the same. And everyone lived happily ever after for a while.

Or, if you want a slightly more prosaic – but plausible – version … the stocking frame was invented in 1589 by William Lee (1550 – 1610). Lee, a clergyman in Nottingham, was said to have developed the machine because a woman whom he was courting showed more interest in knitting than in him.

⇨ Lee's device had a principle of operation that remains in use. Elizabeth refused to grant him a patent because it might put the hand weavers out of business. She was a far-sighted woman.
⇨ In 1663 – sixty years after Elizabeth hopped the Tudor twig – the London Company of Framework Knitters was finally granted a charter. Lee's frame was adapted to use cotton thread but became too expensive for individuals to buy, so wealthy men bought the machines and hired them out to the knitters, providing the materials and buying the finished product.
⇨ In 1734 in Bury, Lancashire, John Kay invented the flying shuttle. This flying shuttle – not to be confused with space shuttles – increased the

---

16. And he wasn't even eligible for a student loan that would have taken 273 years to pay off. Maybe just as well he was ineligible since student loans hadn't been invented.

possible width of cotton cloth and increased the speed of production by a single weaver at a loom.

⇨ Then, in 1759, Jedediah Strutt introduced an attachment for William Lee's stocking frame that produced what became known as the Derby Rib, which opened the door to the mass production of yarn and cloth.

⇨ Resistance by worried workers at that stage of history delayed the widespread introduction of this technology. But resistance was as futile as a sandcastle on the beach or Davy Crockett at the Alamo.[17]

⇨ Builders built houses especially for weavers. They were built over ditches so the weavers could work in a nice damp cellar. It ruined their health, but at least the threads didn't snap. A snapped thread was clearly worse than a dose of pneumonia.

⇨ The weavers were well paid and could earn £2 to £3 a week by the early 1700s. But within a hundred years, machines were replacing them and their wages fell to 12 shillings (60p) a week. Entrepreneurs moved in, as they do, and bought a stock of machines. They then 'employed' cottage weavers to make woven stockings at wholesale prices. Security for the weavers, profits for the bosses.

> *It is a profitable business for the master, but journeymen must have considerable application to earn more than a guinea and a half a week.*
>
> *The Stocking weaver's book* (text from the 1700s)

⇨ In the first seventy years of the 1700s, the wool trade accounted for a quarter of all of Britain's export trade. The masters grew richer and the spinners grew poorer as they worked ever harder. But never mind; it had advantages over being a rural labourer, didn't it?

> *It is, however, clean and neat work, and unexposed to the inclemencies of the weather.*
>
> *The Stocking weaver's book*

⇨ Sweat in a damp room for twelve hours rather than labour in the inclement weather of the fields? The writer omits to mention most of the stocking weavers would have suffered from stoops, short-sightedness,

---

17. Not even John Wayne taking the role of Davy Crockett could prevent the Mexicans overwhelming the Texan defenders. You could say peasant resistance to the Industrial Revolution was bound to Wayne.

chest complaints, and calloused thumbs from the work. They would sometimes work a sixteen-hour day. In the windows were glass spheres containing water and nitric acid, which gave light during the hours of darkness.

⇨ The women made money from spinning. The children grew up knowing nothing other than work. A Victorian reformer rewrote nursery rhymes as 'Sorrowful rhymes' …

> *Jack Sprat had little work,*
> *His wife could get much more.*
> *She and the children worked all day*
> *To keep the wolf from the door.*
>
> Elizabeth Spence Watson (1838–1919),
> social reformer

Urban or rural worker? Which would you choose? The peasants who had revolted against serfdom, and against enclosure, now found themselves trapped in a new sort of slavery for survival.

> *If the workmen do not possess a loom of their own, they allow the master*
> *two shillings a week for the use of his.*[18]
>
> *The Stocking weaver's book*

In addition to the 2-shilling machine rental, the workers had to pay for the machine's upkeep and for breakages. They and their large families lived in inhuman conditions in cramped cottages, *also* rented from the manager, and bought food on site from the manager's grocery stores. It was the same principle as the mediaeval serfs 'paying' their master two days' labour a week on HIS land to earn the right to use THEIR land. Peasants owed their land to the lords; weavers owed their machinery to the masters. They were on piece rate …

> *They are paid so much for each pair of stockings*
>
> *The Stocking weaver's book*

It was a sort of treadmill that you had to keep moving along till you dropped.

---

18. Hang on … looms cost £100 to £150 to buy. There was no question of the stocking weavers buying their own machines.

Did you know ...?

In some ways, the stockingers of the Georgian era were worse off than their peasant forebears. There was an active credit market in many mediaeval towns and villages. Mr and Mrs Peasant could borrow money in the prospect that an investment would pay for itself in increased income – a better plough would give a higher yield. An investment in buildings or livestock would be worthwhile. The stockingers – in a fiercely competitive market – didn't have that sort of aspiration.

Full steam ahead

Caught in the trap of a terrible industrial machinery, harried by a shameful economic cruelty, surrounded with an ugliness and desolation never endured before among men, stunted by a stupid and provincial religion, or by a more stupid and more provincial irreligion, the poor are still by far the sanest, jolliest, and most reliable part of the community.

G.K. Chesterton, in *The Secret People*

In 1762, Matthew Boulton opened the Soho Foundry engineering works in Handsworth, Birmingham. His partnership with Scottish engineer James Watt resulted, in 1775, in the commercial production of the more efficient Watt steam engine, which used a separate condenser.

If the peasant resistance failed to stop the Industrial Revolution in its tracks, then a most unlikely man almost succeeded. Who? Watt ... no, Watt, not what.

James Watt (1736–1819) was a Scottish inventor and mechanical engineer. He took out a cunning patent on his steam engine. Instead of describing it in detail he left it vague:

A new method of lessening the consumption of steam and fuel in fire engines.

So, any other inventor who came up with a 'new method' to improve low-pressure engines was stuffed. They owed Watt a royalty. Watt used his monopoly to amass a fortune.

And Watt passionately opposed the inventors working on a high-pressure steam engine. High pressure would be needed to drive a locomotive on a railway ... and it was the high-pressure railways that transformed the world.

Watt didn't need to invent the locomotive to pay his pension. He was a wealthy man.

Someone tried to have the British Parliament pass an act *banning* high pressure on the grounds that the public would be in danger from such engines exploding.

Who was the man who tried to stop the Industrial Revolution in its tracks? He was an icon of the steam age. Who? Watt. Why?

1. He may have believed his own assertion that high-pressure was dangerous.
2. Or he may simply have seen his massive wealth diminish as his low-pressure engines became as obsolete as a Woolworth's store in a modern high street.
3. But was there another, more personal, reason?

In 1777, Watt had taken his machine to Cornwall to explain how it saved fuel. A Cornish engineer stood up and poured scorn on Watt's claims. Watt was seething. He wrote …

I was so confounded with the impudence, ignorance and overbearing manner of the man that I could make no adequate defence. Indeed, I could scarcely keep my temper which, however, I did to a fault.

James Watt

The impudent and overbearing man's name? Richard Trevithick, sen. The 'ignorant' Cornishman's son, Richard Trevithick, jun., began developing the first truly practical high-pressure steam engine. Was Watt motivated by revenge against the family? Did he mutter, in 1790s' vernacular, 'It's payback time, sunshine'?

Watt's suppression didn't work. Parliament refused to pass the law and Trevithick's high-pressure design triumphed. In fact, high-pressure steam WOULD go on to kill quite a few members of the public, just as Watt predicted. But without high-pressure steam power there'd have been no railway system and the world would have been a different place.

As the railways sprawled in the Victorian era, the upper and middle classes could move out of the smoking, choking towns and their filthy factories. They could afford to commute by train when they needed to visit their workplaces.

The peasants abandoned the country for the town; the middle classes abandoned the town for the country.

Did you know ...?

We mustn't believe the nonsense about Watt inventing steam power after he sat in the kitchen with his aunt, staring at a tea kettle. As the 12-year-old James Watt watched the kettle boil, he had a vision about harnessing the power of that steam. A steam dream

Piffle. Watt himself, in later life, said:

'My attention was first directed in the year 1759 to the subject of steam-engines by the late Dr Robinson ... he at that time threw out the idea of applying the power of the steam-engine to the moving of wheel-carriages, but the idea was not matured.'

March of the machines

Invention, it must be humbly admitted, does not consist in creating out of void, but out of chaos.

Mary Shelley (1797–1851), English author

In 1764, James Hargreaves is credited as inventor of the spinning jenny, which multiplied the spun thread production capacity of a single worker: initially it did the work of eight weavers but in time that increased vastly.[19]

Hargreaves's failure to patent the invention allowed the idea to be exploited by others. That lack of a patent meant there were over 20,000 copies of spinning jennies in use by the time of his death.

One day, Hargreaves's daughter, Jenny (4), accidentally knocked over his spinning wheel. The spindle revolved incessantly and that gave him an idea that a line of spindles could be worked off by just one wheel. (That sudden inspiration probably saved clumsy little Jenny from a clip around the ear.)

In 1764, while Jenny was bumping into spinning wheels, Thorp Mill became the first water-powered cotton mill in the world. It was used for carding cotton. With the spinning and weaving process now mechanised, cotton mills cropped up all over the North West of England. In 1768,

---

19. Trevithick failed to profit from the invention in the way Watt had from the low-pressure machine. Trevithick died in poverty. So did the inventor of the knitting machine, William Lee. Hargreaves was an illiterate spinner and that peasant background didn't help his applications for a patent. The invention thrived; he died a poor man too. Can you see the pattern? There's a message for all of us geniuses. Unfortunately, it's not a very cheerful one.

Hargreaves's house was attacked by a mob from Blackburn who saw the threat of mass production on spinners' jobs and lifestyles.

With the coming of the Industrial Revolution, everything had changed for the peasant – and nothing had changed. In the words of Charles Dickens:

> *It was the spring of hope, it was the winter of despair, we had everything before us, we had nothing before us, we were all going direct to Heaven, we were all going direct to the other way.*
>
> Charles Dickens (1812–1870), English writer
> and social reformer, in *A Tale of Two Cities*

Like Wat Tyler's Peasants' Revolt, the situation was a tinderbox waiting for a spark. It came in 1811.

Peasant protest

> *Where the rich and powerful now have new means to further enrich and empower themselves at the cost of the poorer and weaker, we have a responsibility to protest in the name of universal freedom.*
>
> Nelson Mandela

The invention of steam-powered looms put an end to happy-ever-afters. The machines needed factories and fairly unskilled labour. The cheaper that labour, the bigger the profits. And in the grand old tradition, women and children came cheaper than men.

The textile workers in Nottinghamshire, Yorkshire and Lancashire were skilled artisans who found their livelihoods – families and communities – under threat from a combination of machines and a new, aggressive class of manufacturers who were riding the runaway steam engine known now as the Industrial Revolution.

In Nottinghamshire, in November 1811, the 'framework-knitters' (or 'stockingers') were exposed to wage-cutting. The masters were using cheap youth labour and the new 'wide frames' produced cheaper material. The goods were of inferior quality, but the prices undercut the skilled stockingers. It was a case of (as the London back-street tailors said) 'Never mind the quality, feel the width'.

It wasn't the machines that the stockingers objected to – it was the use of unskilled workers to operate them.

The stockingers were seeing their purses empty and the reputation of their Nottingham craft traduced. In the absence of Robin Hood, a new symbol of peasant rebellion arose: Ned Ludd. And, to reinforce the Robin Hood moral high ground, Ned Ludd came from Sherwood Forest.

Back in 1779, he (allegedly) was one of the first to see the threat of the machines and smashed a couple of them.

In a folk song of 1812 – at the height of the riots in his name – Ludd was hailed as a hero and a reluctant rebel, like William Tell in Switzerland.

> *Brave Ludd was to measures of violence unused*
> *'till his sufferings became so severe*
> *That at last to defend his own interest he rose*
> *And for the great fight did prepare*
>
> The Triumph of General Ludd, traditional song

But even if Ned DID exist, the original story said the song was a wrong song. Ned *wasn't* objecting to the economic misery that the machines brought to the poor. He was retaliating because his master had beaten him. That rather weakens the status of Ned Ludd as a visionary leader, don't you think? Not a man of the people but a man avenging his personal hurt.

Did you know ...?

The Luddite despair of the poor against technology is often seen as contained within a 70-mile swath of northern England from Loughborough in the south to Wakefield in the north. But the mentality of machine-wrecking is more universal. Episodes of machine-breaking occurred in France during the 1789 revolution. You'd have thought the French had more pressing matters than giving looms a kicking?

Their attacks are a delicious irony, since those revolting peasants employed the guillotine machine to decapitate their enemies on an industrial scale.

Ned Ludd's legend inspired ballads of the Robin Hood type ...

> *Chant no more your old rhymes about bold Robin Hood,*
> *His feats I but little admire,*
> *I will sing the Achievements of General Ludd*
> *Now the Hero of Nottinghamshire.*
>
> Ballad

Always keen to protect the masters, the government passed a measure to make machine-breaking a capital offence. An over-reaction that might have shocked even Wat Tyler?

On 10 November 1811, the movement took a sinister turn when John Westley of Arnold was shot dead during a disturbance in Bulwell. His fellow Luddites first removed his body to a safe distance, before returning to the workshop and, 'with a fury irresistible by the power opposed to them', smashed the frames, while the so-called guards all ran away.

The establishment panicked and, as usual, threw violence against the violence. Wellington's army in the Peninsular War was smaller in number than the 12,000 troops assigned to deal with Luddite disturbances in 1812. In Huddersfield alone, 1,000 troops were stationed.

The Luddites succeeded for a long time because government informers failed to penetrate the secret Luddite groups. After all, they were fellow workers and any stranger was immediately suspected of being a spy. One man did succeed in informing on a group and sending three Luddites to the gallows.

But the ingrate authorities refused him the enormous £2,000 reward and he wound up a beggar in London.

Did the Luddite revolts help the peasants' suffering? No more than Wat Tyler's. It made the authorities – on behalf of the 3 per cent of the population who had the vote – react and then overreact. After the crushing of their revolt …

⇨ The factory system, with all its horrors, could no longer be resisted.
⇨ Generations of working-class men and women and children were forced to work twelve hours or more per day for barely a living wage.
⇨ The lives of the workers were regulated by the rhythm of the machines. In the words of a traditional folk song:

> *Up every morning at five,*
> *I wonder that we keep alive.*
> *Tired and yawning, another cold morning*
> *It's back to the dreary old drive.*
>
> *Oh dear, we're going to be late,*
> *Gaffer is stood at the gate;*
> *We're out of pocket, our wages he'll dock it,*
> *We'll have to buy grub on the slate.*
>
> *Poverty Knock*, folk song

… their deaths were often cause by them.

Sometimes a shuttle flies out
And gives some poor woman a clout.
There she lies bleedin', but nobody's heedin';
Who's goin' to carry her out?

Poverty Knock

Reaction to the Luddites established the principle in law that industrialists had the right to continually impose new technology. They could do that without any process of negotiation, either with the people who have to operate the technology or with society at large.

The ugly truth is that this peasants' revolt, as usual, made things worse. They inflicted less violence than they experienced. In one of the bloodiest incidents, in April 1812, around 2,000 protesters marched on a mill near Manchester. The owner ordered his guards to fire into the crowd, killing at least three and wounding a further eighteen. Soldiers killed at least five more the next day.

The machines marched on like H.G. Wells's monsters. Ned Ludd's big mistake? He ought to have invented a machine to destroy the technology faster.

The factories

We must find new lands from which we can easily obtain raw materials
and at the same time exploit the cheap slave labour that is available from
the natives of the colonies. The colonies would also provide a dumping
ground for the surplus goods produced in our factories.

Cecil Rhodes (1853–1902), British statesman

Cecil Rhodes died in 1902 and left money in his will to be spent on expanding the British Empire. He even specified the countries that were ripe for invasion.[20] This magnanimity inspired the verse of the song 'Land of Hope and Glory' …

Wider still and wider shall thy bounds be set;
God, who made thee mighty, make thee mightier yet.

---

20. Rhodes wanted to create a SECRET society that would bring the whole world under British rule. As it's a secret, I'd better not tell you that.

The 'cheap slave labour' of the colonies would provide the raw materials that British factories would turn into profitable goods ... with surplus. How could they achieve this economic miracle? By employing 'cheap slave labour' in the British factories.

This is not some twenty-first-century liberal view. The factory supervisors at the time said it.

> *I work at the silk mill. I am an overlooker and I have to superintend the children at the mill. Their strength goes towards the evening and they get tired. I have been compelled to urge them to work when I knew they could not bear it. I have been disgusted with myself. I felt myself degraded and reduced to the level of a slave-driver.*
>
> William Rastrick, supervisor (interviewed in 1832)

Take the peasants from the fields and put them into the factories. Brutally simple. And the examples are millionfold. Take Robert Blincoe as one example.

At the age of 7, Robert Blincoe grew too large for climbing chimneys so he was returned to the workhouse like some empty milk bottle. He was sent to a cotton mill near Nottingham to work as a 'scavenger' – crawling under the machines to pick up bits of cotton, fourteen hours a day, six days a week.

He was paid with food – he was given porridge and black bread. When he grew weak with hunger, he crept out and stole food from the mill owner's pig troughs. We know about Robert's experiences because he worked his way out of the mills and went on to found his own cotton-spinning business. It's nice to have a happy ending occasionally.

'Scavenging' meant crawling under the machines to pick up the loose cotton from underneath, while it was going. Get your hair caught in the cogs and you are scalped.

> *But accidents frequently occur; and many are the flaxen locks, rudely torn from infant heads, in the process.*
>
> Frances Trollope in *Michael Armstrong: Factory Boy* (1840)

A Report of the Factory Committee denounced the practice. But one factory commissioner was outraged by their report and defended scavenging with a sneer ...

> *The scavengers, who have been said to be 'constantly in a state of grief, always in terror, and every moment they have to spare stretched all*

their length upon the floor in a state of perspiration'. But I have seen scavengers idle for four minutes at a time, and certainly could not find that they displayed any of the symptoms of the condition described in the Report of the Factory Committee.

E.C. Tufnell, factory commissioner

Idle for *four whole minutes* at a time? Mr Tufnell was either in denial … or well paid to contradict the damning Factory Committee account.

Another denier was the journalist Edward Baines …

It is not true to represent the work of the piecers and scavengers as continually straining. None of the work in which children and young persons are engaged in mills require constant attention. It is scarcely possible for any employment to be lighter. The position of the body is not injurious: the children walk about and have the opportunity of frequently sitting if they are so disposed.

Mr Baines didn't volunteer to try scavenging himself. His view is rather at odds with other reports …

On the 6th of March 1865 a very melancholy accident befell a lad named Joseph Foden about 13 years of age. While engaged sweeping under a Mule his head was caught between the Roller beam and the carriage and completely smashed, death being instantaneous.

Quarry Bank Mill record

The mill owners were adamant that the child labourers were essential to the success of the British textile industry. Britain was the world leader, but that would be eroded if the 300,000 little girls were given more time off.

It was asserted by the mill owners that if these little girls worked two hours less per day our manufacturing superiority would depart from us.

William Cobbett (1763–1835), British MP and reformer

When it came to training the factory children, the stick was always preferred to the carrot. One boy in a nail-making factory was punished for making shoddy nails by having his head laid down on an iron counter. And then, a report said …

The boy had a nail hammered through his ear, and the boy has made good nails ever since.

Punishments were part of the life of the factory child. Social reformers complained …

The infants, when first introduced to these abodes of torture, are put at stripping the full spools from the spinning jennies and replacing them with empty spools. Woe be to the child who shall be behind in doing its allotted work. The machine will be started, and the poor child's fingers will be bruised and skinned with the revolving spools. While the children try to catch up to their comrades by doing their work with the speed of the machine running, the brutal overlooker will frequently beat them unmercifully, and I have frequently seen them strike the children, knocking them off their stools and sending them spinning several feet on the greasy floor.

Samuel Fielden, social reformer,
Lancashire (commenting in 1877)

'Spinning several feet' was the least of their pain. Orphaned Jonathan Saville was sold as a pauper apprentice to a master in a textile industry. His master threatened to 'knock out his brains' if he did not get up to work, and pushed him to the ground, breaking his thigh. Eventually, bent double and crippled, he was returned to the workhouse, no longer any use to the master. Or slave-master. Surely Cecil Rhodes would have approved?

Whose fault was it? The government? The factory owners? God and his angels? No. The parents (if you care to believe one apologist).

The opinions of two medical gentlemen of Manchester, with whom I have conversed upon the subject of factories and health, come to this: that the insalubrity of Manchester and of the Manchester operatives is occasioned not by the labour of the mills, but by the defective domestic arrangements for cleanliness and ventilation.

Angus Reach, *The Morning Chronicle* (1849)

'Defective domestic arrangements for cleanliness and ventilation'? Or dirty homes? Oh, the joys of sesquipedalian verbiage.

Five ways to kill a kid

If the factories and the mines didn't kill you before your teens, then there were other perils lurking in the peasant past …

1. Mudlarks

Some London children made their living by collecting anything valuable that wound up in the river Thames. They usually waited for low tide before they waded through mud to sort through the river deposits. Mudlarks were mostly young boys, though girls and old women knee-deep could be seen there too. It was exhausting work for little reward – a mudlark could hope to find coal, scrap metal, and firewood. Finding coins or anything valuable was a rarity. The two main dangers were: the 'toshers' – the men who hunted in the filth of the sewers and who weren't gentle in snatching your finds; and any small wound picked up while wading in the poisonous mud. A cut could equal a death sentence.

2. Crossing sweepers

Taking a brush and cleaning up road crossings and pavements for wealthy people sounds harmless enough. There's always the chance of a tip. But apart from being scragged by rival sweepers, the droppings and urine of the horses created an unhealthy miasma. The odd dead horse added to the hazard. (You couldn't flog it.) Apart from the diseases, the crossing sweepers were always in danger of accidents; panicking horses lashing out, or just careless drivers running you over. A hansom reward for doing a useful job?

3. Glassmakers

Like mill workers, children involved in glassmaking faced serious injuries and fatalities every day. Bosses sneered at these 'dog boys' or 'blower's dogs' – because they were trained to follow the adult glass-blower's whistle. The children handled and cleaned every piece of molten glass that the glass-blower took from the furnace. As they were on a piece rate, they worked as fast as they could and paid the price for careless haste. In one accident, a 14-year-old boy was permanently blinded in one eye after being struck by a piece of flying glass. 'Blow-overs', or glass dust, caused extreme pain once it got into the lungs or the eyes. Burns and dehydration were common, of course, but so were tuberculosis and pneumonia. The latter was the result of working in intense heat and then walking home on a cold winter's night.

4. Powder monkeys

Children weren't recruited for the army but in the Georgian era they could join the navy from the age of 12. (Horatio Nelson did that and ended up on a column.) On a Royal Navy warship then they faced all the dangers of fighting seamen and more. As well as cabin boys like the fictional Jim Hawkins (Aharr, Jim lad), small boys were useful at bringing gunpowder for the cannon. Obviously, you couldn't keep the gunpowder handy on the deck in a battle as the risk of an explosion was great. It was kept below deck, where the risk was less. A bit. Powder monkeys were invariably recruited from the poorer classes, and their task was to scurry from powder keg to gunners as fast as they could. The job didn't always appeal, so sometimes boys had to be pressed into service by the navy. Pauper parents were happy to hand over their skinny (but nimble) offspring to get them off the list of mouths to feed.

5. Matchmakers

Making matches involved dipping the wooden sticks into phosphorus … the explosive bit on the end. Prolonged contact with poisonous white phosphorus was the cause of phossy jaw – phosphorus necrosis of the jaw. Fumes from the phosphorus into which matches were dipped ate at their jawbones, leaving them with empty cheeks that oozed foul-smelling liquid, brain damage and eventually death from organ failure. The disease could rip off a girl's jaw – they were usually girls – and lead to a massive infection and a slow, painful death. For once, peasants revolting was successful. A group of girls working in a London factory held a strike in 1888 and were successful in getting concessions from their employers, including replacing white phosphorus with the safer red phosphorus. Matchmakers, like Bryant and May, paid dividends of 38 per cent. Rich shareholders saw £5 shares rise to nearly £19. That profit did not take into account the cost in terms of matchgirl misery.[21] In 1891, the Salvation Army opened up its own match factory using red phosphorus and paying better wages. But there were still

---

21. A fine of three pence for talking was deducted from the eight pence daily wage. This translated into profits for shareholders, of course. Mr Bryant took twelve pence from each girl's wage as their contribution to a statue for the lovely Mr Gladstone PM. Many matchgirls went to the unveiling of the statue with stones and bricks in their pockets. Later they surrounded the statue and a gruesome story is told that some cut their arms and let their blood trickle on the marble paid for by their blood. Did Bryant's partner, Mr May, not want a statue for Mrs May?

young homeworkers using white phosphorus to their cost. Several younger children in their families died from eating these matches.

The matchgirls' success gave the working class a new awareness of their power, and unions sprang up in industries where unskilled workers had previously remained unorganised.

London's East End was certainly the epicentre of this new militancy; however, the matchgirls' strike inspired workers nationwide. Their courage, fighting spirit and resolution also inspired the middle-class suffragettes of the following decades.

Tolpuddle Martyrs

God is our guide! From field, from wave,
From plough, from anvil, and from loom;
We come, our country's rights to save,
And speak a tyrant faction's doom:
We raise the watch-word liberty;
We will, we will, we will be free.

George Loveless, Tolpuddle Society member

It wasn't just the *industrial* peasants who were revolting. In 1833, the agricultural labourers of the early 1800s were as defiant as Wat Tyler had been 500 years before – but less violent in their protest.

Labourers' wages were falling – they'd been reduced to 7 shillings a week with the threat of a further drop to 6 shillings. The labourers of Tolpuddle in Dorset said they'd not work for less than 10 shillings. They formed a mutual help society – effectively, a trades union – with a creepy initiation ...

⇨ The image of a skeleton was painted.
⇨ The new member would be blindfolded and invited to swear their allegiance.
⇨ The blindfold was removed, and the painting presented to him.
⇨ The skeleton was a reminder of human frailty but ...
⇨ ... also, a threat as to what might happen if they betrayed the society.

(At this point, a bad punster would call them a highly skulled workforce, but you'd not read such trivia here.)

A local landowner/magistrate was outraged by the peasant presumption and wrote to the Home Secretary, Lord Melbourne, demanding action. But laws against such organisations had been repealed. Melbourne came up with an outrageous (and devious) suggestion: charge the six leading men under an old and unused law, the Unlawful Oaths Act 1797.

That skeleton initiation ceremony – not worthy of a student fresher-week lark – fitted the bill. (Or the Unlawful Oaths bill fitted them up.)

> *There is no crueller tyranny than that which is perpetuated under the shield of law and in the name of justice.*
>
> Montesquieu (1689–1755), French philosopher

They were arrested and tried and found guilty. The sentence was transportation to Australia for seven years.

After the sentence was pronounced, the working class rose up in support of the martyrs. A massive demonstration marched through London and an 800,000-strong petition was delivered to Parliament protesting about their sentence. Some said it was the first British protest march. (Maybe they were forgetting Wat Tyler's Peasants' Revolt and a few other uprisings.)

After three years, the government (and a new Home Secretary) relented and the men returned home with free pardons and as heroes.

But they lost three years of their lives and suffered a lot of distress.

James Brine (1813–1902) gave an example of the hardships. In Australia he was robbed of all the bedding, clothes and (importantly) shoes allocated by the authorities on his way to his assigned master.

> *I was employed to dig post-holes … having walked so far without shoes, my feet were so cut and sore I could not put them to the spade. I got a piece of an iron hoop and wrapped round my foot to tread upon, and for six months … I went without shoes, clothes, or bedding, and lay on the bare ground at night. Shortly afterwards I was sent to the pool to wash sheep, and for seventeen days was working up to my breast in water. I thus caught a severe cold and having told my master that I was very ill, asked him if he would be so good as to give me some-thing to cover me at night, if it were only a piece of horse-cloth.*

That master had believed the fake news that preceded the arrival of the martyrs. He was sure they were terrorists out to steal the very clothes off the backs of their masters. He told Brine …

> *'No,' said he, 'I will give you nothing until you are due for it. What would your masters in England have had to cover them if you had not been*

sent here? I understand it was your intention to have murdered, burnt, and destroyed everything before you, and you are sent over here to be severely punished, and no mercy shall be shown you.'

They didn't exactly want to murder, burn or destroy. They wanted 10 shillings a week.

The working-class martyrs of Tolpuddle returned to Britain as national heroes. But to the Dorset landowners they were a threat to their wealth and comfort. They forced five of the six returning convicts to seek new lives in Canada, where they settled as farmers in London, Ontario.

James Hammett alone returned to Tolpuddle. How did the country treat this hero of the working classes? Hammett died in the Dorchester workhouse in 1891. A bit of a clue there as to the answer.

Karl Marx would have praised the martyrdom of the Tolpuddle workers.

Religion is the sigh of the oppressed creature, the heart of a heartless world, and the soul of soulless conditions. It is the opium of the people.

Karl Marx (1818–1883), German political theorist

But old Karl was wrong about that – as he was about most things. The opium that allows workers to release their energies, their frustrations and their grievances – rather than channel them into revolting – isn't religion. You don't go to church for a knees-up.

It is entertainment …

Chapter 2

Entertainment

Bad laws are the worst sort of tyranny.
Edmund Burke (1729–1797), Irish statesman,
in a speech at the Bristol election of 1780

And the worst sort of bad laws are the ones that apply to the poor but not to the rich. The world of entertainment seems an unlikely source of injustice, yet peasants have suffered it.

Take the Cornish 'gentleman' William Carnsew, who lived in the 1500s. He played bowls, quoits and card games.

However, playing these games had been against the law for almost everyone ever since the Middle Ages. Kings had forbidden people from playing games in order to force them to practice archery. In 1542, Henry VIII revived the laws that banned …

all artificers, husbandmen, labourers, mariners, fishermen, watermen, servants and apprentices from playing Backgammon, cards, dice, football, bowls, Tennis, ninepins and shove-groat.[1]

So how did Carnsew get away with it? Because he was a member of the gentry, with an annual income of more than £100. The underclasses could only play those games at Christmas … and then only in their own home. The penalty for flouting that law was a fine of £1. Which illustrates the old proverb about different laws for rich and poor.

Laws grind the poor, and rich men rule the law.
Oliver Goldsmith (1730–1774), Irish novelist
and playwright, in *The Traveller* (pub. 1764)

---

1. A groat, as you probably know, was worth four old pence. It was introduced back in the days of Edward I in the 1270s. What you may not know is that it was still being minted in Britain as late as 1856, and groats were still being minted in British Guiana (Guyana now) until 1955. And, by the way, shove-groat isn't a misprint for shove-*goat*, which is a different game altogether. No kidding.

Plough thy neighbour

> *Heck, what's a little extortion among friends?*
> Bill Watterson (b. 1958), American cartoonist

It can be hard going back to work after a holiday. So, it is understandable that mediaeval peasants enjoyed a little work avoidance in the form of primitive theatre.

Plough Monday (the first Monday after 6 January) was the day the labourers went back to their fields after the Christmas break. The Christmas break had followed Advent – a time of fasting – with a time of gluttony. For lucky peasants with generous lords it could be a time for charity and sharing food – at Christmas in 1314, some tenants at North Curry in Somerset received loaves of bread, beef and bacon with mustard, chicken soup, cheese and as much beer as they could drink for the day.

After that excess, as you may imagine, they delayed the evil hour of the return to work. One excuse was the little light entertainment of Plough Monday – or Bully-thy-neighbour.

The peasant labourers toured the village, carrying their ploughs, singing and dancing for money. They covered their faces in soot and went from door to door asking for money.

> *A pageant consisting of a number of sword dancers dragging a plough, with music; one, sometimes two, in very strange attire; the Bessy, in the grotesque habit of an old woman, and the Fool, almost covered with skins, a hairy cap on, and the tail of some animal hanging from his back. The office of one of these characters, is to go about rattling a box amongst the spectators of the dance, in which he receives their little donations.*
> John Brand, in *Observations on Popular Antiquities* (1777)

You were at liberty to refuse, of course. But, if you did, there was every chance your garden would be ploughed. Trick or treat? And you thought Halloween extortion was a modern phenomenon?

The tricksters could not be recognised because of their blackened faces. (Don't try this 'trick' scam next Plough Monday or that blackened face could get you 'treated' to a spell in one of HM Prisons.)

Did you know ...?

The word Christmas was first recorded in 1038. Goodness knows what Santa and his elves did before that. Around 1400, people started decorating their houses and churches with green plants. And a new Christmas curse arose – carol singers. Children from poor families started visiting houses of rich people at Christmas and they sang Christmas carols. You have to wonder if they were greeted with the warmth of Mr Scrooge and a cheery 'If I could work my will, every idiot who goes about with "Merry Christmas" on his lips should be boiled with his own pudding and buried with a stake of holly through his heart.'

Savage sport

He who is cruel to animals becomes hard also in his dealings with men. We can judge the heart of a man by his treatment of animals.

Immanuel Kant (1724–1804), German philosopher

The Middle Ages drew to a close and the feudal system had crumbled.[2] Landowners began to enclose common ground – with the consent of their friends in Parliament – and the common land that sustained the peasant class was closed to them.

Enclosure (when all the sophistications are allowed for) was a plain enough case of class robbery.

E.P. Thompson (1924–1993), British historian

The peasants were driven to the larger towns to find work. They became 'waged' and had leisure time (and maybe some spare cash) for their entertainments. The homegrown amusements became professional.

Animal rights among the peasantry were non-existent. The cruel indifference to animal suffering was carried into the towns and enjoying the torture, or slow death, of animals was regarded as 'sport'.

---

2. Historians enjoy a neat closure. They generally agree that the Middle Ages ended with the last great charge of knights down Ambion Hill at the Battle of Bosworth Field in 1485. Richard III was hacked to death by Henry Tudor's rebel army. Of course, nothing is ever that clean cut. The nearest Richard's enemies came to clean cuts were two to the inferior aspect of his skull – sharp force traumas – possibly from a sword or a halberd.

Bearbaiting

For as long as men massacre animals, they will kill each other. Indeed, he who sows the seed of murder and pain cannot reap joy and love.

Pythagoras (d. 495 BC), Greek philosopher

From Tudor times, bears were kept for baiting. Specialist arenas were built: bear gardens. They usually comprised a high fenced area, around 'the pit', and raised seating for spectators.

A post would be set in the ground towards the edge of the pit and the bear chained to it, either by the leg or neck. Several dogs, usually Old English Bulldogs, would then be set on it. As they grew tired (wounded or killed) they were replaced. Sometimes the bear was let loose and allowed to chase after animals or people.

It wasn't a peasant sport as such – lords enjoyed it as much as the underclasses – but it was the literate classes that recorded the 'pleasures' of the sport. Queen Elizabeth's favourite, Robert Dudley, Earl of Leicester, told of an event at Kenilworth Castle in 1575 …

Well, the bears were brought forth into the court, the dogs set to them, to argue the points even face to face. Very fierce, both one and the other, and eager in argument. If the dog in pleading would pluck the bear by the throat, the bear with traverse would claw him again by the scalp but could not avoid it.

Therefore, with fending & proving, with plucking and tugging, scratching and biting, by plain tooth and nail on one side and the other, such expense of blood and leather was there between them, as a month's licking (I think) will not recover.

Yes, Robert, but weren't you disgusted? He went on (as if in answer to our query) …

It was a very pleasant sport, of these beasts, to see the bear with his pink eyes leering after his enemies' approach, the nimbleness and waiting of the dog to take his advantage, and the force and experience of the bear again to avoid the assaults. If he were bitten in one place, how he would pinch in another to get free, that if he were taken once, then what shift, with biting, with clawing, with roaring, tossing and tumbling, he would work to wind himself free from them. And when he was loose, to shake his ears twice or thrice with the blood and the slather about his face, was a matter of goodly relief.

That's all right then. A couple of shakes of his ears and he was right as rain … a very red rain.

If you were bored with the same-old, same-old dog attacks then the whipping of a blinded bear offered some variety.

On at least one occasion, a pony with an ape tied to its back was baited. A witness reported …

The screaming of the ape, beholding the curs hanging from the ears and neck of the pony, is very laughable.

Not everyone in Tudor Britain was enjoying the laughs. A stand that collapsed at the Paris Gardens on 12 January 1583 resulted in the deaths of several spectators.[3]

This was clear evidence, said the Puritans, that God was angry. It wasn't so much the suffering of the animals, but the fact that the bearbaiting was taking place on a Sunday. A more cynical observer would say …

The puritan hated bear baiting, not because it gave pain to the bear, but because it gave pleasure to the spectators.

Thomas Babington Macaulay (1800–1859),
British historian and politician

Bullbaiting and more

In the courtyards of inns there was cockfighting, dogfighting and bullbaiting too.[4] The bull had pepper blown into its nostrils to make him fighting mad. It was placed in a hollow in the ring and trained dogs were sent, one at a time, to fasten their teeth into the bull's snout.

As with so much cruelty, the perpetrators were able to justify their actions. 'Baiting the bull before killing it makes the flesh more tender,' they claimed as they polished their haloes.

In 1584, a foreign visitor to the bear garden described the cheerful little scene …

There is a round building three stories high in which are kept about a hundred large English dogs, with separate wooden kennels for each for

---

3. It gives a twisted - but literal – meaning to the phrase 'They died laughing'.
4. One of London's prime cockfighting pits was at 10 Downing Street. Make up your own joke from that factoid.

them. These dogs were made to fight one at a time with three bears, the second bear being larger than the first and the third larger than the second. After this a horse was brought in and chased by the dogs and, at the end, a bull who defended himself bravely.

Baiting was finally outlawed by the Cruelty to Animals Act of 1835, which 'forbade the keeping of any house, pit, or other place for baiting'.

However, rat baiting was not banned, and ratting competitions grew more popular as a gambling sport. At one time, in Victoria's London, there were at least seventy rat pits.

This was a rather dirty, small place, in the middle of the Cambridge Circus, London. You went down a rotten wooden stair and entered a large, underground cellar. It was full of smoke, stench of rats, dogs, and dirty human beings as well. The stale smell of flat beer was almost overpowering. Gas lights illuminated the centre of the cellar, a ring enclosed by wood barriers. This was the pit for dog fights, cockfights, and rat killing. A hundred rats were put in it; large wagers went back and forth on whose dog could kill the most rats within a minute. The dogs worked in exemplary fashion, a grip, a toss, and it was all over for the rat. With especially skilful dogs, two dead rats flew through the air at the same time.

James Wentworth Day (1899–1983), British writer

The bloodlust of the British was imaginative – especially when it has been possible to gamble on the result.

In 1874 a dwarf was set to fight a bulldog. In the 11th round the dwarf had knocked the dog unconscious but suffered considerable injuries in the process.

and …

In Georgian times there was duck-baiting. A duck with trimmed wings was sent into a pond and dogs took it in turns to swim out and catch it. The dog that caught the prey fastest was the winner.

Duck-baiting? Unbelievable … but true.

Power plays

Bearbaiting was a popular and profitable 'sport' for the organisers. The trouble was, the bears needed a rest every other day. What could the bear pit owners do to entertain the Elizabethans on the bears' day off? Give them plays.

> *I can take any empty space and call it a bare stage. A man walks across this empty space, whilst someone else is watching him, and this is all that is needed for an act of theatre to be engaged.*
>
> Peter Brook (b. 1925), theatre director, in *The Empty Space*

The later Tudor age is famous for its theatre. Writers like Kit Marlowe (1564–1593), Ben Jonson (1572–1637) and William Shakespeare (1564–1616) began to create plays that are still performed around the world. Queen Elizabeth and King James were fans. But the theatres couldn't have survived without the underclasses paying their penny to stand and watch – the 'groundlings' … no prizes for guessing how they got that name.

The bear-pit entrepreneurs wanted to give the groundlings a bit of the old glamour and guts of the mediaeval religious plays. Sword fights and deaths drove audiences to Shakespeare's *Romeo and Juliet*, blood and murder to his *Macbeth*, devils and ghosts to Marlowe's *Doctor Faustus* and themes of trickery and money to Jonson's *The Devil is an Ass*.

But where did these great plays come from? Did William Shakespeare just sit down one day and say 'I am going to write a great play'?

In the Middle Ages the workers in the towns had produced religious plays, often based on Bible stories. But they weren't just a way of preaching to people on stage. They were exciting, shocking and frequently so tasteless they'd be shown after the watershed on modern television. They featured …

⇨ devils springing from trapdoors
⇨ God and his angels swooping down from cranes
⇨ Hell's mouth opening and belching out smoke
⇨ floods, fires and earthquakes being recreated
⇨ characters suffering gory executions and wounds
⇨ animals like rabbits and rams appearing for sacrifices.

The costumes and masks were dazzling; the singing and dancing loud and lively. They were created by the working-class guilds for the working-class citizens.

It was a Catholic tradition and Henry VIII's chopping and changing of the Church put a stop to much of it. The peasants were deprived of their holy-day excitement.

Art is so wonderfully irrational, exuberantly pointless, but necessary all the same. Pointless and yet necessary, that's hard for a puritan to understand.

Gunter Grass (1927–2015), German novelist

New plays were needed, but the playwrights couldn't give the audiences the religion of those old plays – doing religion could get you hanged, burned and chopped in Tudor times.

Instead they looked back to the traditions of the Roman theatre. They took ideas from a writer like Seneca. And his favourite subjects were crime and revenge, witches and ghosts, and they were very popular. The Romans loved tales of horror. Shakespeare probably read Seneca's gruesome plays at school.

William Shakespeare was a clever man. When he started writing at the end of the 1580s, he was going to give the bear-garden mob the sort of fun they wanted ... he was going to give them horror.

If the plays of Marlowe, Kyd and Shakespeare were written today they would struggle to find a producer brave enough to stage them. But in Tudor times, theatres sprang up to accommodate the new development of the old art.

These theatres were full of groundlings on the floor in front of the stage ... with a few of the posh patrons sitting in the private boxes or on the stage. They demanded to be entertained. It was the peasant groundlings who drove the great age of theatre. It's grim to think that the emerging theatre owed its existence to the animal cruelty – a day off for the baited bears.

History is about as instructive to us as an abattoir.

Seamus Heaney (1939–2013), Irish poet

In the civilised world of the twenty-first century, baiting is illegal, and bears are scarce. But it still goes on with other innocent animals. The bait these days can be stolen pets, puppies, kittens, rabbits, small dogs. Some of these animals are obtained from 'free to good home' adverts.

A bait animal's teeth may also be broken to prevent them from fighting back and if the bait animal is still alive after the event, they will be given to the dogs as a reward, and the dogs finish killing them.

Plus ça change, plus c'est la même chose.
(The more things change, the more they continue to be the same thing.)

Jean-Baptiste Alphonse Karr (1808–1890),
French journalist and novelist

Eviscerating entertainment

All the world loves a clown.[5]

Cole Porter (1891–1964), American composer

If you couldn't afford the penny for the theatre, then the entertainment could come to you – in the street.

There were street entertainers in the towns doing spectacular things for money. There were entertainers who swallowed swords. We've all seen that. But one man took the sword-jeopardy a step further: he pretended to stab himself in the stomach. The audience witnessed blood gushing from the wound.

As you can guess, it was a trick; he had a bag of pig's blood under his shirt and a wooden shield under that. When he stabbed himself, the pig's blood spurted out and the audience gasped with wonder (or threw up in terror). One drunken entertainer forgot the wooden shield one day, so when he stabbed himself in the stomach he died. Human nature being what it is, we can be sure some of the audience thought that was the best trick they'd ever seen.

A juggler called Kingsfield showed the body of 'John the Baptist', who'd had his head cut off – the head lay at the feet of the 'corpse' and it spoke.[6]

Then there were 'visitor attractions' to separate the customers from their hard-earned pennies. One popular tourist destination was Sir Francis Drake's circumnavigation ship, the *Golden Hind*. It was on display at Greenwich. Typically, the ship was quickly destroyed because most visitors took a piece as a souvenir. By 1618, only the keel was left.

When we destroy something created by man, we call it vandalism but when we destroy something by nature, we call it progress.

Ed Begley, junior (b. 1949), American actor

---

5. Not true, as any Coulrophobic will tell you.
6. We don't know what John the Baptist's head said as it lay next to his feet. Maybe something along the lines of, 'I wish I'd washed me socks.'

For those who couldn't afford admission to the *Golden Hind*, you could see (in 1581) a Dutch giant over 7 feet 6 inches tall and dwarf 3 feet high. A fully-grown live camel was on display in a house on London Bridge in 1599.

The most popular free sights of the City of London were the public ceremonies and processions. Many featured Queen Elizabeth I, who liked to awe her peasants with the sight of her jewelled gowns. The common people have a bizarre curiosity about what members of the royal family are wearing. Perhaps they feel more regal if they wear a dress that Duchess Grizelda wore to Prince Cyril's christening? You'd have to ask them.

Weedy wonder

Ods me, I marvel what pleasure of felicity they have in taking their roguish tobacco. It is good for nothing but to choke a man and fill him full of smoke and embers.

Ben Jonson, in *Every Man in His Humour*

As you'd expect, drinking was a popular pastime, but a new habit developed during Elizabeth's reign. Smoking became popular after 1573, when William Harrison wrote about it in his book *English Chronology*. It wasn't called smoking at this time; it was called 'drinking the smoke'.

The custom spread among the working classes despite warnings from their superiors …

A custom loathsome to the eye, hateful to the nose, harmful to the brain, dangerous to the lungs, and in the black, stinking fume thereof nearest resembling the horrible Stygian smoke of the pit that is bottomless.

James I of England (1566–1625), in
A Counterblaste to Tobacco (1604)

It would be 400 years before the world listened to James.

Vile Victoriana

Cruelty, like every other vice, requires no motive outside of itself; it only requires opportunity.

Mary Anne Evans (1819–1880, pen name George Eliot),
English novelist

Street entertainment for peasants down the centuries could be revolting and cruel. One hundred and fifty years ago, people were still enjoying 'laugh-at-the-freak' shows at the fairs.

The Hyde Park Fair in the 1860s presented a spectacular to celebrate Queen Victoria's thirty years on the throne.

On the bill were 'The Talented pigs' and 'The ponies that tell your fortune'. These were standard circus fare, but others were less tasteful and included:

⇨ the world's fattest man
⇨ Miss Scott – the two-headed lady
⇨ Yorkshire Jack – the Living Skeleton
⇨ the world's spottiest boys.

Did you know ...?

Madame Stevens – the Pig-faced Lady – was especially sad. Now you may wonder what people really saw when they paid to see Madame Stevens, the Pig-faced Lady? They saw ...

⇨ a bear that had its face and paws shaved to look like pink skin
⇨ paws laced into padded gloves
⇨ the animal strapped to a chair with a table in front of it.

Then the performance began. The bear was asked questions. A boy prodded it with a stick after each question. The bear grunted and that seemed to be a reply ...

'Are you 18 years old?' (Prod – Grunt.)
'Is it true you were born in Preston in Lancashire?' (Prod – Grunt.)
'Are you well and happy?' (Prod – Grunt.)
'Are you planning to get married?' (Prod – Grunt.)

But this was too cruel even for the Victorians and when the fair reached Clerkenwell, it was banned.

It was clearly an 'unofficial' celebration of Victoria's thirty years on the throne. The Clerkenwell audiences must have moaned, 'We are not amused'.

Chapter 3

Courtship

Marriage is good for those who are afraid to sleep alone at night.

Saint Jerome (347–420), hermit[1]

To be a peasant, in any age, was to be underprivileged. To be a woman peasant was to be so far under underprivileged she probably wouldn't be able to spell it.

Why this inequality? Because men had been making the laws for millennia.

You must make women count as much as men; you must have an equal standard of morals; and the only way to enforce that is through giving women political power so that you can get that equal moral standard registered in the laws of the country. It is the only way.

Emmeline Pankhurst (1858–1928), British political activist

Daughters-in-law

In the history of love and marriage, the women were often seen as chattels to be traded by fathers and owned by husbands.

The greedy father did marry his young and dainty daughter to a miser of filthy, tawny, deformed and unseemly hue; so wretched and ill-favoured a creature, as repugnant to reason, or any manner of considerate and wise thought.

Angel Day (1586), Elizabethan scholar, in *The English Secretary*

---

1. Old Jerome was a curmudgeonly hermit. Would you accept marriage guidance from this sort of man? But if grouchy Jerome can become a saint then there's hope for the rest of us … well, for me at any rate.

These fathers took a lead from their aristocratic 'betters', of course. King Henry I of England (1068–1135) betrothed his 7-year-old daughter, Matilda, to Holy Roman Emperor Henry V, who was 28.

Daughters were offered with a sum of money – a dowry – to get them off their father's hands. It was paid to the groom's family. The father 'gave away' his daughter – a form of words still available – with the offer …

I give thee my daughter, to be thy honour and thy wife, to keep thy keeps and to share with thee bed and goods.

But there were also deals whereby the bride could be bought. King Canute (995–1035) said that if a woman's husband died she had to stay a widow for twelve months. If she married within the year, the bride would have to pay back the purchase price to the dead groom's family. Henry I made this law of Canute part of the fabric of his English marital legal system.

Dads worried that pre-marital sex (and the risk of pregnancy) was taboo, so the simplest solution was to marry off the girl when she reached puberty – at 12 to 14. Does your daughter suffer from teenage hormonal swings? Sex will 'cure' her, they believed.

Spot your spouse

Match. Chat. Date.

Slogan for internet dating site

Despite dictatorial dads, young singles had dreams of romantic partnerships. They were impatient and didn't want to wait for love to find them. They wanted to KNOW who their true love would be, and they wanted to know NOW. They used a multitude of techniques that didn't require a smartphone app and a Wi-Fi connection.

Here are a handful of tried and tested that even a peasant can use:

WARNING: Will Shakespeare parodied these magical meetings in A Midsummer Night's Dream *when Titania was subject to a charm that would make her fall for the first thing she met when she awoke. She fell for the peasant weaver, Bottom, who happened to have an ass's head at the time. Be warned, young love-seeker, and don't blame me if you try the following spouse-spotting techniques and fall for next-door's Rottweiler, your brother/sister's geeky friend or a passing traffic warden.*

1. First, fill your mouth with water and grab an entire handful of salt. Go outside and walk around the house three times. If you succeed in doing this without swallowing any water or spilling any salt, you will find your future spouse in the first person you meet.
2. Peel a Pippin apple, making one long, unbroken apple peeling. Swing the peeling around your head three times and let it drop to the floor. If it forms a letter, it will be the initial of your future spouse. As you peel the apple and swing the paring, repeat the following lines:

   > *Pare this pipping round and round again,*
   > *My sweetheart's name to flourish on the plain.*
   > *I fling the unbroken paring o'er my head,*
   > *My sweetheart's letter on the ground is read.*[2]

3. Should a virgin wish to know if she'll be married in the year, she should go out to the chicken coop on Christmas Eve and knock on the door. If she hears a rooster crow, she will marry. If she hears a hen cluck, she won't.
4. A wedding tradition (that's still practised widely) dates as far back as the 1300s in England. Single female wedding guests would literally tear away pieces of the bride's dress and bouquet in the hope that some of her luck in love would transfer to them. Usually, the bride would just throw her entire bouquet to the guests so that she could get away. With time, this became the bouquet-toss that we know today, and it's now believed that the woman who catches it will be the next one to marry. Unlike the Pippin peeling practice, it doesn't give you clues as to WHO you will marry.
5. Take a piece of wedding cake home, sleep with it under your pillow (or under your bed) and you're sure to dream of your future spouse. And if you don't dream, then at least you get to eat the (slightly squashed) cake, so what do you have to lose?

To wit to woo

But, before marriage, there came courtship. Winning the love of your life was the first problem. Persuading someone to love your average face and dubious habits may require some help.

---

2. The Celtic druids were said to have read the future from sheep or chicken guts spilt on the ground. The Archbishop of Canterbury, Thomas Becket, was still consulting a gut-reader as late as the 1160s. Saint Tom ended up murdered on his cathedral floor. He didn't see that one coming. He should have stuck to Pippins.

Did you know ...?

According to a research institute in Gangtok, Sikkim, the first known aphrodisiac was body odour.

Peasants – men and women – had body odour by the bucketful. The lucky people. The rich hid their odour with baths and perfumes. Famously, Queen Elizabeth I said ...

> *I take a bath four times a year ... whether I need to or not.*

Until the twentieth century, few households in the developed world had indoor piped supplies. Instead, water was fetched from a well in the garden, a pump in the street, or a nearby stream. Time-consuming and exhausting.

The rich had their servants to do the donkey work. Inevitably, much less water was used by the rural peasants, for whom a bath was a labour of lather. The result was lower standards of personal peasant hygiene.

Even by the 1800s, the middle classes were little better. You may think a dance would suffocate you with perfume. But, in fact, it would be body odour, as one Georgian diarist recorded ...

> *We could hardly breathe it was so hot and the smell was beyond anything.*
> Harriet Wynne (1786–1860), diary (1805)

Many mediaeval rural peasants may have never bathed, though their equals in the towns usually had a bath house.[3]

Aphrodisiac additives

Europeans of the Renaissance swore by asparagus as an aphrodisiac, and the church banned it from nunneries.[4]

Anonymous historian

---

3. It was said that a peasant could expect to be fully bathed just twice in his/her life; once, when they were born and when they had died. They would appreciate neither

4. Health warning: eating asparagus causes gas and makes urine smell of bad eggs. That just may counteract the aphrodisiac effect for some. Then again, there's no accounting for taste ... or smell.

After you've identified your lover with a little magic, you now need to raise their ardour.

The legendary lover Casanova had a diet of fifty oysters for breakfast. Not usually an option for peasants. So, where else could they turn for an aphrodisiac?

Here are some of the foods that people in the past thought would make someone fall in love with you. Just remember …

No one has ever succeeded at seduction by means of food alone.
Manuel Vázquez Montalbán (1939–2003),
Spanish writer, in *Immoral Recipes*

Lovers have been known to feed their listless and lustless partners …

⇨ the brains of sparrows (and their tongues)
⇨ ambergris (from the guts of a whale)[5]
⇨ charred newt
⇨ flesh from a foal's forehead
⇨ walnuts (in 1300s Europe … because they resembled testicles)
⇨ rabbit penis
⇨ bat's blood
⇨ goat or stag testicles boiled in milk.

Gathering any (or all) of these ingredients – apart from the walnuts – could land you in prison these days and put paid to your amorous adventures.

One love potion that seemingly *did* work on men, like today's Viagra, was known as Spanish Fly. It was made from the crushed dried bodies of green blister beetles. British peasants would not have had access to this, which is probably just as well. It can cause kidney malfunction or gastrointestinal haemorrhages.[6]

Great injury befalls those who take the Spanish Fly, because they will feel a burning corrosion in almost all their body. … They will suffer from

---

5. A waxy substance excreted by sperm whales, mainly through defecation but sometimes through vomiting. Good luck with that one. Elizabeth I wore it around her neck in a pomander and she was legendary for NOT getting a lot of love action. Maybe spare yourself the expense of an XXXL fishing rod to catch your whale?

6. French soldiers of the 1800s who feasted on frogs that had themselves been dining on green blister beetles.

swoons, surfeit, and light-headedness, and will fall to the floor and gnaw table legs.

Antonio Gamoneda (b. 1931), *The Book of Poisons*

And no lover is going to welcome your kisses when your mouth is full of chair-leg splinters.

Of course, if you enjoy something *too* much then the government will ban it. Many aphrodisiacs were banned in the Middle Ages. Herbs and spices like basil, mint, cinnamon, cardamom, ginger, pepper, saffron and vanilla were forbidden during mediaeval times because they were often used in love potions.

All nonsense? Even today, reputable websites like 'BBC Good Food' offer pages of 'Aphrodisiac recipes'.[7]

What if a man is TOO passionate, ladies? An old cure says you must take a pot of his urine and drown a lizard in the liquid. That will turn him as limp as ... well ... the dead lizard. It offers no suggestions on how you extract the urine.

Paying the price

Women are systematically degraded by receiving the trivial attentions which men think it manly to pay to the sex, when, in fact, men are insultingly supporting their own superiority.

Mary Wollstonecraft (1759–1797), in
A Vindication of the Rights of Woman

Prostitution, famously, is the world's oldest profession ... though Eve's job as an apple picker ought to qualify.

Before the days of the brothel, the prostitutes in the Jewish scriptures seemed to work from home. Women like Rahab, the prostitute in Jericho who aided the spies of Joshua, advertised her house with a scarlet rope.[8]

There was a Christian ambivalence towards the brothel in the Middle Ages – the Church had the urge to license and to regulate to prevent the greater evils of rape and sodomy. No lesser figures than Saint Augustine

---

7. Maybe the Trade Descriptions Act doesn't apply to the BBC?
8. Some say the origin of the 'red light'. Others argue ingeniously that it came from the red lanterns carried by railroad workers left outside brothels while they were inside. But why would the workers (a) leave their lanterns burning, and (b) leave them outside?

and Saint Thomas Aquinas argued that prostitution was a necessary evil: a well-ordered city needed brothels just as it needed good sewers.

> *Prostitution in the towns is like the cesspool in the palace; take away the cesspool and the palace will become a dirty and stinking place.*
>
> Saint Thomas Aquinas (1225–1274), Italian Dominican friar and philosopher

The prostitutes in brothels were invariably women from the underclasses. Famous diarist and Samuel Johnson biographer James Boswell (1740–1795) excused his liaisons with prostitutes because they were from the lower classes …

> *I went to the park, picked up a low Brimstone and agreed with her for Sixpence, went to the bottom of the park, arm in arm, and dipped my machine in the Canal, and performed most manfully.*

His own 'performance' was deemed worth recording by this literary paragon. The feelings of the 'low Brimstone' were not.[9]

If most prostitutes were working-class women, then their team managers were men. But not always the sort of shadowy men you'd imagine. In London, Southwark was the red-light district. Brothels, usually whitewashed, were called 'stews' because of their origins as steam bathhouses.

Prostitutes were active in the theatres. Theatrical impresarios and actors, such as Philip Henslowe and his son-in-law, Edward Alleyn, owned a profitable brothel. There is a (plausible but unprovable) theory that their star turn, William Shakespeare, died after he caught syphilis from his time in the London brothels.

But there was a more powerful landlord of the mediaeval London brothels. The Catholic Church … no doubt following the precepts of Thomas Aquinas.

Many of London's mediaeval brothels were located in the part of Southwark owned by the Bishop of Winchester. In 1161, a parliament of Henry II introduced regulations allowing the bishop to license brothels and prostitutes in the area, which became known as the 'Liberty of the Clink'. It

---

9. Boswell was so addicted, he continued these liaisons despite contracting gonorrhoea at least nineteen times in his life.

was a partnership between state and Church. Male-dominated institutions providing a service for males.

Prisons are built with stones of law; brothels with bricks of religion.
William Blake (1757–1827), English poet and painter

With such a blessing from God and the king, brothels thrived. The bishop was their landlord, and they were often shut down when Parliament was in session to keep up appearances. Records of court cases show that priests, monks and friars were among their clients.

The brothels had to allow weekly searches by constables and the bishop could not charge prostitutes more than 14 pence per week for a room … and there was no VAT chargeable as it hadn't been invented. (The lawmakers missed a trick there.)

The rules said that prostitutes were not allowed to live at the brothels or to be married, and they were required to spend a full night with their clients. 'Ladies of the night' meant the full night … though there was no Trade Descriptions Act to enforce this.

How could the Church condone prostitution? They had Thomas Aquinas's blessing as well as his fellow saint, Augustine, who argued bottled-up lust would lead to violence …

Suppress prostitution, and capricious lusts will overthrow society.
Saint Augustine (354–430), Roman theologian

Then they had the precedent of Mary Magdalene, a 'sinful' follower of Jesus whose reputation and memory was widely (but wrongly) denigrated as a prostitute. And, of course, the brothels were operated by low-born women who were chattels rather than human souls headed for Heaven … in fact, when they died, they were thought to be buried in un-consecrated ground. We must assume that when they reached the gates of Heaven, Saint Peter would turn them away with a saintly 'Go to Hell'.

But the biggest justification of the Church's involvement? It made the bishops a nice fat profit to indulge their earthly avarice.

In 1310, Edward II ordered the abolition of London's brothels but it can't have been very effective as Henry VIII, in 1546, was obliged to close the bawdy houses to prevent the spread of disease. His belief would be echoed by a fellow psychopath 400 years later …

The fight against syphilis demands a fight against prostitution.
Adolf Hitler (1889–1945), German fascist leader

The Tudor prostitutes were referred to as 'dissolute and miserable persons'.[10] Even Fat Hen had little success in stopping the trade ... some of the houses were moated and had high walls to repel law enforcers.

Rules were set in place in London and other cities. Brothels were situated in special streets. Men in religious orders and married men were forbidden to visit. Prostitutes, in distinctive dress, were allowed to trade just outside the town walls but not inside – though inner areas like Covent Garden in London were hotbeds of the profession. Special houses were built for prostitutes who wished to repent – a neat piece of double-think by the Catholic Church.

> *We say that slavery has vanished from European civilization, but this is not true. Slavery still exists, but now it applies only to women and its name is prostitution.*
>
> Victor Hugo (1802–1885), French novelist, in *Les Misérables*

And the good news in the mediaeval days of licensed brothels? They were not allowed to open on holidays.

So, we have to hope the ladies had a well-earned rest. A sort of bunk holiday.

To babe or not to babe

> *No woman can call herself free who does not own and control her body. No woman can call herself free until she can choose consciously whether she will or will not be a mother.*
>
> Margaret Sanger (1879–1966), American nurse and sex education activist

Under the Bastardy Act of 1733, any poor, pregnant, unmarried woman was obliged on oath to name the father, who was then arrested and forced to marry her. In January 1787, a Norfolk clergyman, James Woodforde, wrote:

> *Rode to Ringland this morning and married one Robert Astick and Elizabeth Howlett by licence, the man being in custody, the woman being with child by him. The man was a long time before he could be prevailed on to marry her when in the churchyard; and at the altar behaved very unbecoming.*

---

10. 'Miserable', perhaps, but only 'dissolute' if you were looking for an excuse to ban them.

We can only guess at reluctant Rob's 'unbecoming' behaviour at the altar.

'Do you take this woman?'

'Nope.'

'Do you take this woman ... or else.'

'Oh, all right then.'

Not the greatest start to married life. But that bastardy law had more deadly consequences in Norfolk's southern neighbour, Suffolk.

Murderous marriage

Laws are no longer made by a rational process of public discussion; they are made by a process of blackmail and intimidation, and they are executed in the same manner.

H.L. Mencken (1880–1956), American journalist

You can understand the theory behind the Bastardy Act. 'Name the father. He can support the child and remove the burden from society and the workhouse.' But, in practice, it opened a door to murder.

The case of John and Sarah Nichols, Honington, Suffolk, 1794

To a father growing old nothing is dearer than a daughter.

Euripides (480–406 BC), Greek poet

The Bastardy Act failed to take into account the cases where the father COULD NOT marry the mother ... even if she revealed his identity. Look at the case of John, Sarah and Nathan Nichols.

The murder was so very brutal, the judge enforced the 1752 law: the Horrible Murder Act. It allowed him to sentence the guilty party to be dissected by the surgeons and/or have their hanged corpses displayed in an iron cage – a gibbet. As he passed sentence the judge said ...

The murder you have committed is of a most aggravated and extraordinary nature; that a father should aid and abet his own son in murdering a daughter is an instance of depravity I have never before witnessed in the office I now hold; and I sincerely hope I never shall again.

John Nichols was a brutal peasant in rural Suffolk and inflicted his bullying on the children from his three marriages. One Saturday evening, he sent 16-year-old Sarah a mile to fetch 3 stone of flour for the house. That was

Did you know …?

The gibbet inspired one of France's great poets, François Villon, to write a cheerful ditty from the point of view of the criminal …

> *Human brothers who come after us,*
> *Don't harden your hearts against us.*
> *The rain has washed away our filth,*
> *The sun has dried and blackened us.*
> *Magpie and crows have scratched out our eyes*
> *And torn our beards and eyebrows.*
> *We are never still, but sway to and fro in the wind.*
> *Birds peck at us more than needles on a thimble.*
> *Brothers, there's no laughter in this.*
> *May God absolve us all.*

suspicious in itself because his latest wife (it was later revealed) had enough flour in her kitchen.

Half an hour later, John set off with his son Nathan in the footsteps of young Sarah. They would meet the girl on her way home as she staggered along the dark country lane.[11] John pulled a fence post from a nearby quarry and told young Nathan to beat Sarah with it when they met.

Sarah appeared, and Nathan struck her about the head and body till she fell senseless to the ground. The father and son fled the scene, but then John had second thoughts. He sent Nathan back to take a garter off the dead girl and wrap it tightly round her throat to make it look as if she'd strangled herself.[12] Sarah's body was half-hidden in a ditch, where it was seen the following morning.

The trail of evidence led to John and young Nathan and they were hanged; Nathan's body was sent to the surgeons for dissection while father John had his corpse displayed in an iron gibbet till it rotted.[13]

---

11. I don't know about you, but I'd stagger under the weight of 3 stones of flour.
12. Yes, the historical and criminal examples of girls strangling themselves with their own garters are somewhere between nil and zero. Girls strangling themselves after beating themselves over the head with a fence post are not recorded. But we can guess our panicking pair were none too blessed with brain cells.
13. The gibbet was later discovered and put on display in a Bury St Edmunds museum (Moyse's Hall), where, to this day, ghouls may go and see it. There was no corpse left inside the iron cage … only John Nichols's boots. (We can guess the heels would be fine but his sole had gone to Hell.)

Over thirty witnesses gave evidence against the murderers. But NO ONE mentioned MOTIVE. The prosecution lawyers and the judge never touched on the subject. Why on earth would John order Nathan to kill his sister?

The peasants of Honington knew. Folk wisdom said Sarah discovered she was pregnant and would be compelled under the Bastardy Law to name the father then marry him. But the father was Nathan, the locals said.

> *Try everything once except incest and folk dancing.*
>
> Thomas Beecham (1879–1961), British conductor

It seemed Nathan had tried one – if not both. Marriage was not an option. The family were hanged if she told, hanged if she didn't … figuratively speaking. And hanged if they silenced her … literally.

The Bastardy Law caused as much misery as it sought to avoid.

> *People get in auto accidents, they're paralyzed for life. I got hurt worse getting married.*
>
> Jake LaMotta (1922–2017), American athlete

As many as fifty babies are abandoned in the UK each year, with some dying from cold or exposure before they are discovered. The mediaeval age had ways of dealing with unwanted children that some saw as humane.

Peasant families could find an extra mouth too much to cope with. Some newborns were left in a place where they could be found and raised by childless couples. Some mediaeval churches had what were called 'foundling wheels' – round windows through which unwanted babies could be passed. Even in the Middle Ages, there was opposition to the custom.

> *Children are cast into a cloister by their parents or relatives just as if they were kittens or piglets.*
>
> William of Auvergne, Bishop of Paris

Other were taken to a local monastery to be raised in the religious institution. And those monasteries made baby leaving easier by installing a custom-built box at their gates. Parents could put their unwanted baby there as if it were a large letterbox, knowing it would be sheltered … and the monks or nuns could be happier knowing they wouldn't trip over some little bundle in the dark.[14]

---

14. If it had been an electronic age, a baby boy could have been announced with an alert saying, 'You've got male'.

The idea of a baby postbox was revived in 2013. Campaigners called for the introduction of 'baby hatches' in hospitals or public buildings across the UK where desperate mothers could leave their children in safety. The call came after a baby girl was found abandoned on a park bench in Edinburgh.

A campaigner was herself abandoned, and argued …

I had no blanket, I was in a pillowcase and I was literally hours old. I had mild hypothermia. If I hadn't been found when I was, another hour or so and I would have been a statistic.[15]

Henry VIII's dissolution of the monasteries removed this baby box facility and unloved children were vulnerable to a more grisly fate at the hands of a 'baby farmer' – a woman paid to raise the child, for a fee. And once the parent stopped paying, it wasn't in the interests of the baby farmer to keep the child alive.

Using the monasteries as informal adoption agencies was perhaps a kinder way to deal with the timeless problem. It was invariably the woman's problem.

it is not only unfair but disgustingly cruel that the mother is always held responsible for the illegitimate child, while the father goes scot-free.
Dale Evans (1912–2001), American actress and singer

Mediaeval marriage

Marriage is neither heaven nor hell, it is simply purgatory.
Abraham Lincoln (1809–1865), American President

⇨ The church tried to control marriage, but in the Middle Ages, couples did not need to marry in a church for it to be binding. Records show people getting married on the road, down the local tavern, round at a friend's house or in bed. All that was needed for a lawful marriage was the consent of the couple involved.

⇨ There was no formula ceremony … 'Do you take … sickness and in health … joined in holy deadlock' etc. Our buxom brides needed no witnesses because God is the ultimate witness and she knows all.[16]

---

15. However, under current UK law it is illegal to abandon a child. Don't do it. Not even if the child in question is a stroppy teenager who refuses to tidy their bedroom.
16. By Tudor times, the bride undertook to obey her husband and the word 'buxom' meant 'obedient'. Down the years it seems to have changed to mean physically well-endowed.

⇨ Having sex created a legally binding marriage. Consent could also be shown by giving and receiving an item known as a 'wed'. A 'wed' could be any gift but was often a ring. In a Tudor engagement, William Hanwell gave two pennies to give to Isabel and they were hitched. A 'wedding', where a man gave a woman a ring and she accepted, created the marriage. But beware, lustful swains ...

> *No man should place a ring of reeds or another material, vile or precious, on a young woman's hands in jest, so that he might more easily fornicate with them, lest, while he thinks himself to be joking, he pledge himself to the burdens of matrimony.*
>
> Statute of the English Church (1217)

Interesting, is it not, that the church sees marriage as a 'burden'?

> *Thus grief still treads upon the heels of pleasure:*
> *Married in haste, we may repent at leisure.*
>
> William Congreve (1670–1729), English playwright,
> in *The Old Batchelour*

⇨ 'Marry in haste, repent at leisure' was never more true than for people of the Middle Ages. Divorce, as we understand it today, did not exist. The only way to end a marriage was to prove it had not legally existed in the first place. So, a Tudor warning was designed to be read out in church ... after which it's surprising anyone wanted to marry ... ever ...

> *There are few marriages without chidings, brawlings, tauntings, repentings, bitter cursings, and fightings.*
>
> *An Homily of the State of Matrimony* (1563)

⇨ Sex outside of marriage was a sin. Christians could marry from puberty onwards; at the time that was 12 for women and 14 for men. Parental consent was not required. That didn't change until the 1700s. But the no-nookie rule was widely ignored; a third of Elizabethan brides were pregnant by the time they came to church.

⇨ Couples who were already related were not permitted to marry. The definition of 'incest' before 1215 covered any couples with a great-great-great-great-great-grandparent in common. A church ruling in 1215 reduced that to having a great-great-grandparent in common. But godparents and godchildren were not allowed to marry as they were 'spiritually' related, and 'in-laws' were also prohibited from marrying.

⇨ Marriage between people of different classes was especially frowned upon. Marriage between people of the same gender was unthought-of. As an actor said …

> *I think that gay marriage should be between a man and a woman.*
>
> Arnold Schwarzenegger (b. 1947), American politician
> and former professional bodybuilder[17]

Marital misery

> *If your husband is a drunkard who abuses, then you must be playful and appeal to the goodness in him. Do NOT empty a full chamber pot over his head.*
>
> Desiderius Erasmus (1466–1536), Dutch philosopher,
> in *Praise of Marriage* (1519)

So, Erasmus was saying a woman ought NOT to empty the family's human waste over a man's head. That means some women must have DONE it at some time.

The marriage guidance books like Erasmus's, written for the upper classes, would not have been read by the peasantry, but they reflect the attitudes of the time. It's fair to assume the underclasses held similar values. In which case, the advice to men was simple: behave yourself.

The church flowed the precepts of the Bible:

> *And I say unto you, Whosoever shall put away his wife, except it be for fornication, and shall marry another, committeth adultery.*
>
> King James Bible, Matthew 19:9

The mediaeval Church occasionally granted a divorce. In 1442, they allowed John and Margaret Colwell to separate.

> *They swore they would rather prefer death in prison to living together.*

---

17. Maybe the muscles in the body were developed at the expense of the muscles in the brain. Or maybe Arnie's views are so profound and metaphysical, it is we mere mortals who fail to understand his wisdom?

The civil law of Britain was just as dismissive of women who suffered abusive marriages. In 1805, a woman petitioned Parliament to divorce her husband. He lived openly with his mistress and children. The High Chancellor, Lord Eldon, heard her case and said she was the most admirable plaintiff he had ever heard in his court. BUT ...

However hard the divorce laws may press on a few individuals, it would on the whole be better if no bill of this kind were passed.

So, His Lordship agreed adultery was a bad thing, but allowing it as an excuse for a woman to divorce was a worse thing.

Between 1801 and 1857, there were just four women granted divorces.[18] Caroline, wife of The Honourable George Norton, failed after a protracted legal struggle. In the underclasses, the wives of abusive men didn't even have the divorce option. It was 'Stand by your man' ... or nothing.

Charles Dickens portrayed the abusive man with the fictional character Bill Sikes in *Oliver Twist*. You'd hope the world would have moved on. But a hundred years after Dickens's death, the musical version of *Oliver Twist* still had the abused, a working-class woman, singing ...

Who else would love him still,
When they've been used so ill?
He knows I always will
As long as he needs me

The blame game

In ancient times, women were blamed for unhappy marriages, never men ...

Call no man unhappy until he is married.

Socrates (470–399 BC), Athenian philosopher

Misogyny never decreased through the ages. Always the insistence that men were the victims. A married man was obliged to have and to hold till death do one-or-the-other part. And men resented that 'death-do-us-part' prohibition, even though many had promised it in the wedding ceremony.

---

18. As opposed to Henry VIII, who managed two divorces in seven years ... or four divorces if you count a couple of beheadings as a quickie divorce?

They found support for demonising women in the Bible …

> *All wickedness is but little to the wickedness of a woman: let the portion of a sinner fall upon her.*
>
> King James Bible, Ecclesiasticus 25:19

The bitter men who wanted to renege on marriage vows found solace in writers who whinged that a wife curtails a man's liberty …

> *Any young man who enjoys the delights of the world finds marriage a narrow and sorrowful prison cell, full of tears, torment and grieving. He who throws himself into it has lost his mind.*
>
> *Five Joys of Marriage*, French book (1400)

And the reason? Women have 'longings', and if a man doesn't satisfy them then she will find someone who will …

> *If a husband can't her needs supply,*
> *Adultery's the way she'll try.*
> *Her lustful loins are never stilled,*
> *By just one man she's unfulfilled.*
> *She'll spread her legs to all the men,*
> *But, ever hungry, won't say 'When'.*
>
> *Against marrying*, Anonymous (1225–1250)

And, having betrayed the foolish man who has ignored this advice, the woman will let him raise the resulting child …

> *Thus, bitter grief and shame begin;*
> *The child that's been conceived in sin.*
> *Its mother knows its bastard line.*
> *The foolish husband says: 'It's mine'.*

Marital advice to women is recorded in folk songs. And its guidance seems to be to choose a husband rather like you would choose a horse, for its fitness …

> *An old man came courting me, hey ding dooram day*
> *An old man came courting me, me being young*
> *An old man came courting me, all for to marry me*

Courtship

Maids, when you're young never wed an old man
Because he's got no faloorum, fadidle eye-oorum
He's got no faloorum, fadidle all day
He's got no faloorum, he's lost his ding doorum
Oh Maids When You're Young, Never Wed An Old Man

It seems like tongue-in-cheek advice. Yet the misogyny – the woman to blame – creeps into later verses and betrays the old male fears of the wife straying …

When he went to sleep, out of bed I did creep
Into the arms of a handsome young man
And I found his faloorum, fadidle eye-oorum
I found his faloorum, fadidle all day
I found his faloorum, he got my ding doorum
So maids when you're young never wed an old man

Traditional British folk song

A 1967 recording of that song was banned by the BBC because they said it had sexual themes. Did the censors see smut in the young man's 'faloorum' or the woman's 'ding-doorum'? Surely not. Those BBC people must have had very dirty minds if they saw anything perverted in an innocent piece of marriage guidance.

Chapter 4

Sickness

On average, a boy born in one of the most affluent areas will outlive one born in one of the poorest by 8.4 years.

Longevity Science Panel (quoted on BBC website, 15 February 2018)

So, peasants don't live so long as their rich contemporaries. That's bad news. But it gets worse: seventeen years before the 2018 report, the gap was just 7.2 years. The difference had increased by 1.8 years. (By 2120, the gap should be fifteen years … all other things being equal.)

'Twas ever thus. The rich get richer and the poor get deader.

Duirt mé leat go raibh mé breoite. (Irish for 'I told you I was ill'.)[1]

Epitaph on gravestone of Spike Milligan (1918–2002), Anglo-Irish comedian

You don't need the Longevity Science Panel to tell you that the rich have a better diet, better living conditions and less stressful physical work. You can't imagine Richard III going down a colliery and coming out to proclaim, 'Now is the winter of our discontent made warm as summer by this coal of York.'

In such condition [where] there is no place for industry … the life of man, [would be] solitary, poor, nasty, brutish, and short.

Thomas Hobbes (1588–1679), English philosopher, in *Leviathan*[2]

---

1. The local church authorities refused to allow 'I told you I was ill' on the headstone. Milligan had it written in Irish and it was allowed. The headstone was removed to allow the interment of his wife and sadly never replaced. If we can't laugh at death, then what can we laugh at?
2. The full title is *Leviathan or The Matter, Forme and Power of a Common-Wealth Ecclesiasticall and Civil*. But you don't need to know that so I won't mention it.

Death was a little more democratic in the Middle Ages. When Death and his fellow horsemen of the Apocalypse rode out, they brought Famine, War and Conquest. But Conquest is sometimes known as Pestilence. And Pestilence struck without asking to see your bank balance.

The Mortality

Neither physicians nor medicines were effective. Whether because these illnesses were previously unknown or because physicians had not previously studied them, there seemed to be no cure. There was such a fear that no one seemed to know what to do. When it took hold in a house, it often happened that no one remained who had not died. And it was not just that men and women died, but even sentient animals died. Dogs, cats, chickens, oxen, donkeys, and sheep showed the same symptoms and died of the same disease. And almost none, or very few, who showed these symptoms, were cured. The symptoms were the following: a bubo in the groin, where the thigh meets the trunk; or a small swelling under the armpit; sudden fever; spitting blood and saliva (and no one who spat blood survived it). It was such a frightful thing that when it got into a house, as was said, no one remained. Frightened people abandoned the house and fled to another.

Marchione di Coppo Stefani (1336–1385), Italian statesman

At the time the Black Death struck Britain, in 1349, it was known as 'The Mortality', or 'The Pestilence', not 'The Black Death'.

The Mortality wasn't too fussy about who it killed. But children were especially vulnerable … a priest explained …

It may be that children suffer heaven's revenge because they miss going to church or because they despise their fathers and mothers. God kills children with the plague – as you can see every day – because, according to the old law, children who are rebels (or disobedient to their parents) are punished by death.

Other religious experts blamed human lust – the sin of Adam …

God often strikes us, to test our patience and justly punish our sins. But is to be feared that the most likely explanation is that human sensuality – that fire which blazed up as a result of Adam's sin – has now plumbed greater depths of evil, producing a multitude of sins which have provoked the divine anger, by a just judgement, to this revenge.

Bishop Edendon of Winchester (d. 1366)

The rich had the option of leaving the infested towns and retreating into their relatively clean country houses. The peasants had to stay and suffer.

The statistics are appalling but if you were surrounded by the dead and dying you were more concerned with your own fate. The faces of the peasants, and the face of the land, changed.

And into these places every joy has ceased; pleasant sounds are hushed, and every note of gladness is banished. They have become abodes of horror and a very wilderness; fruitful country places without the tillers are deserts and abandoned to barrenness.

Bishop Edendon of Winchester

You'd know if you felt the signs of oncoming plague: a feeling of sudden coldness, pins and needles, fatigue and depression. Then the swellings in the groin and/or armpit – 'buboes', which gave the name to Bubonic Plague. You see a discolouration of the skin and little blisters elsewhere on the body.

Then you wait to die ... or to recover. You have a fifty-fifty chance.

But if the symptoms included breathing difficulties and the coughing up of blood, then you have Pneumonic Plague, and that is 90 per cent fatal.[3]

Imagine your desperation. The priests (the ones who survive) will pray for your soul in the next world. But, to be honest, you'd rather not depart this world for another few years ... another fifty years will do. So, you turn to the doctors and will give everything you have to buy their remedies.

And for once, poor peasant, you are on a level playing field with the rich. There were cures for millionaires and cures for paupers. The prices varied, but the efficacy was the same. They were all rubbish.

Plague came to Britain and the world was never the same.

> *The world is changed and overthrown*
> *That it is well-nigh upside-down*
> *Compared with days of long ago.*
>
> John Gower (1330–1408), English poet

---

3. If the infection gets into your bloodstream it becomes septicaemic plague and the survival rate is zero, zippo and zilch. Write your will while you still can – or if you're an illiterate peasant, dictate it to a monk.

Crazy cures

The best doctor is the one you run to and can't find.
Denis Diderot (1713–1784), French philosopher

The mediaeval peasant-hypochondriac had a fair range of revolting diseases to choose from … but a far smaller range of cures that worked. The hypochondriac could enjoy dysentery, typhoid fever, cholera and diarrhoea – mainly due to dirty water and foods infected by bacteria. Many people thought these diseases were caused by eating raw fruits and vegetables, so they suffered scurvy from avoiding the very healthy foods that would save them.

Skin diseases like measles, smallpox and chicken pox caused scarring of skin, blisters, high fevers and, in some cases, death.

Mediaeval doctors had no idea what caused the plague, but would tell you it was the result of:

⇨ the movements of the planets
⇨ a punishment from God
⇨ bad smells and corrupt air
⇨ enemies who had poisoned the wells[4]
⇨ staring at a victim
⇨ wearing pointed shoes
⇨ strangers in your town or village.[5]

The doctors

Doctors are men who prescribe medicines of which they know little, to cure diseases of which they know less, in human beings of whom they know nothing.

François-Marie Voltaire (1694–1778), French philosopher

You have a choice of medics to help you depending on where you live and what you can afford. Five different names … or maybe ONE name …

---

4. In France they said the English did the poisoning; in Spain they blamed the Arabs. In Germany, suspected poisoners were nailed into barrels and thrown into the river. And everyone blamed lepers.
5. When the Mortality struck Bristol – at 10,000 people, the second largest city in Britain at the time – the citizens fled to Gloucester. The good folk of their neighbours, Gloucester closed the gates on them to avoid catching the Mortality. An early 'I'm alright Jack' mentality. It didn't work.

QUACKSALVER: *a person who pretends, professionally or publicly, to skill, knowledge, or qualifications he or she does not possess; a charlatan.*
Dictionary

1. The Physician

He will check the patient's urine and pulse to decide on the best treatment. He boasts of being able to treat chills, fevers, skin and stomach complaints, with his services in demand in all the great households.

He will tell you …

I have been to university and I stand for book learning, particularly as it relates to astrology, the theory of the humours, and uroscopy.

As for the Pestilence, he will tell you …

Plague is the result of corrupted air (a 'miasma') entering the body and creating a poisonous imbalance of the body's humours (of which there are four: blood, phlegm, yellow bile, black bile).

This corruption came about at the conjunction of Mars, Saturn and Jupiter in Aquarius, whose effect was magnified by a total eclipse of the moon on 18 March in 1345. Anyone born under the sign of one of these three planets will be more susceptible to the disease.

I recommend a medicine made of dittany, pimpernel, tormentil and scabious, blended in cold water: to be taken by the spoonful six times daily.

He will require payment for his medicine and will be the most expensive option available. He may choose to deliver his services while holding a vinegar-soaked sponge in his teeth: this is to act as a barrier against the corrupt air exhaled by the patient.

But, if your purse can stand it, he will flog you a box of crushed emerald. One spoonful a day – for a large sum of money – will cure you. (And if it doesn't then you'll be too dead to ask for your money back.)[6]

Not a medic for the peasants.

---

6. I've never tried to grind an emerald to powder, but I suspect it must be tricky with mediaeval technology. You just have to suspect the 'ground emeralds' were powdered glass from an old bottle. Don't try that at home … even if you get pins and needles and believe the Mortality has struck you while you are reading this book.

2. The Apothecary

(or 'spicer')
He will tell you …

> *I'm a merchant, so I know all of the very latest medicines available on the open market and can source the best quality ingredients from trusted suppliers. I see all sorts of people with all sorts of complaints in my shop. I can find you the ingredient that you need and there is no one else so well versed in the hidden virtues of plants, stones and animal parts.*

As for the Pestilence, he will tell you …

> *A miasma is the cause. In other words, unpleasant smells. Miasma is produced by stagnant water, cesspits and rotting meat, or is carried to England from foreign parts by warm, southerly winds: it is essential that windows be shut when the wind is in this direction. Prevention is better than cure, and the house should be cleaned and sprinkled with vinegar, roses and vine leaves, all of which can be purchased from me. Burning spices and juniper branches is also an effective way of fumigating the house. Available in my shop, for a small payment, naturally.*

The apothecary can also make a wax plaster for the buboes: this contains seeds of rue and oil of camomile, amongst other herbs, which allegedly draw the poison out of the body and away from the vital organs, neutralising it.

The apothecary will only consult with you, the patient, while holding a nosegay to ward off the bad miasma.

Cheaper than the Physician … but will you trust a man who prescribes arsenic as a medicine?

3. The Barber-surgeon

He will tell you …

> *I've had 'on-the-job' training via an apprenticeship, between the ages of 14 and 21, as in any other craft. I've satisfied all of the conditions needed to be admitted to a guild, including a strict examination by the guild members, I know my astrological and lunar charts so I know the best times to administer my treatments. As well as cutting hair and shaving beards, a barber-surgeon is permitted to carry out surgery, setting bones,*

tooth extractions, bloodletting and lancing boils. I also use the wax from votive candles in church, to cast in the shape of your painful body parts. You can offer that model at a shrine in the hope of getting a cure.

As for the Pestilence, he will tell you …

I am an expert in bleeding to release the excess of blood in your body. The blood, which is a hot humour, is causing you to overheat. At an early stage of infection (when the pins-and-needles prickling of the skin is first felt) I will release corrupt matter from the body by making an incision and letting out blood. Of course, it would also be very unwise to draw blood if the moon is in conjunction with that body part's corresponding zodiacal house. For instance, if the moon appears in Libra, it would be dangerous to cut anywhere near the patient's lower back, hips, or kidneys. Bleeding, if done correctly, can relieve all kinds of ills, including headaches, frenzy, giddiness, blindness, swellings, breathing difficulties and an irregular heartbeat.

Monks had to shave the tops of their heads and that created a job opportunity for barbers. They were armed with razors and that, in turn, made them handy of a battlefield – amputating mangled limbs. Physicians were not keen on surgery, so they sub-contracted a lot of the bleeding work to their local barbers. Sometimes the barber-surgeons employed leeches to suck out the blood.

Did you know …?

Often, leech collectors were older peasants with no other way to make money, so many of them used their own legs as bait. They stood in a leech-filled bog and waited for the pinches. The leeches do not take a great deal of blood in a feed, but the wounds that they create can bleed for ten hours or more. It would be a desperate peasant who made a living this way.

The trade of the barber-surgeon expanded to include the removal of cataracts, midwifery, pulling teeth, performing enemas and pig gelding.

Blood-letting was invariably harmful to the patient. If you avoided a barber-surgeon's attentions, could you be said to have had a close shave?

Bleeding too much, as you will know, is fatal. In the traditional tale of Robin Hood, the outlaw was bled by the devious Prioress of Kirklees. The balladeer enjoyed recounting his fate ...

> *At first it bled the thick, thick blood*
> *And afterwards the thin,*
> *And well then knew, good Robin Hood*
> *Treason was there within.*

Start with a man full of blood, bleed him, and then there was nun.

4. The Monk

He will tell you ...

> *You peasants will usually turn to your nearest monastery where there will be a hospital. More important than treatments for the body, however, is the cure of the soul. Upon arrival at the hospital, you must make a confession and do penance, so that your priest can give you absolution. Prayers to the hospital's patron saint in its chapel will also help on the road to spiritual recovery. Bless you.*

As for the Pestilence, he will tell you ...

> *The monks will attend to your physical needs, if you become too disabled to feed, move or wash yourself. We will pray for you, and we will admonish you for unchristian behaviour. We offer no cure, except to see you more safely on your way to the Almighty, by praying for you now and after your death. Our prayers will help to speed you through purgatory, the state that awaits you after your death, and that can be even more painful than your pestilence, before your cleansed soul can ascend to Heaven.*

The monastic hospital usually made sure that the bedding was clean and valued fresh air and work: only the very sickest were permitted to 'eat the bread of idleness'. At least they would have done you less harm than the ones who bled you and fed you 'medicines' of the day.

And if you had the Pestilence, the monastery would ensure you died in comfort. Never forget, the Mortality can be a blessing from God: it reminds you that earthly joy is fleeting, and it takes the innocent out of the way of sin.

5. The cunning woman

Cunning Women were professional or semi-professional practitioners of magic in Britain. They mainly used spells and charms as a part of their occupation. Their magic would be used to neutralise malevolent witchcraft, to locate criminals, missing persons or stolen property, for fortune telling, for healing, for treasure hunting and to influence people to fall in love.

She will tell you …

I am the wise woman of the village and I do my best to help my neighbours with their problems. They come to me to detect thieves, find lost items, hunt for treasure and tell their fortunes. And cures, of course. A love potion for you, sir? For something like toothache I'll bring you the five-leaved herb, cinquefoil. Of course I gather this only between the twenty-third day of the Moon up until the thirtieth day, and only for the hour of Mercury on each day. You can hear me singing about your toothache as I go about my gathering so. I squeeze out the juice of the herb and give it to you to hold in your mouth. I'm a lot cheaper than the other so the peasants love me. Yes, some jealous people accuse me of witchcraft. They would 'swim' me … throw me in the river with my thumbs tied to my big toes.

As for the Pestilence, she will tell you …

Do you have those pins and needles that foretell the Pestilence? Then I'll offer you the flesh of a hedgehog. They are prickly, so their flesh might be consumed to block the prickling sensations of the Pestilence. Or the blood of hares can be used. A hare can outrun a swift disease, and with its help so can you. I might also prescribe some herbal remedies for poultices or plasters on your plague spots, using herbs that correspond with with heavenly bodies. But the best cure is to take a live chicken, shave its bottom and place the shaved area on the purple boils. The chicken bottom draws out the poison from the plague sore. It never fails.

The best way to scientifically test the efficacy of their peasant cures is to try one on yourself. Next time you have a headache, take incense from your local priest, mix it with pigeon droppings and wheat flour; mix it with the white of an egg and bandage it to whereso the head acheth. It shall vanish anon.[7]

---

7. If symptoms persist – and you haven't died from a fungus in pigeon droppings called Cryptococcus – please consult your doctor.

If you know (and loathe) someone with a cut that has become infected then you may like to offer them the following cure from a leechbook of the 1400s:

A right good powder for fester: take a toad or an adder and a weasel or a mole and a cock-raven and burn them in a new pot. When they are turned to powder put it in the fester.

Daily dangers

It is true greatness to have in one the frailty of a man and the security of a god.

Lucius Seneca (5 BC–AD 65), Roman statesman

Life is brief, but for peasants it was more greasy pole than leisurely stroll. Death with his scythe was in every shadow of every corner. He was always there when you didn't expect him as well as (in plague times) when you did.

Look at the tricks he had up his voluminous sleeve …

1. Brutal births

It is easier to find men who will volunteer to die, than to find those who are willing to endure pain with patience.

Julius Caesar (100–44 BC), Roman general and historian

Ancient Roman fake news said that the term 'caesarean' was derived from the surgical birth of Julius Caesar. This seems unlikely since his mother, Aurelia, appears to have lived to hear of her son's invasion of Britain. At that time the procedure was performed only when the mother was dead or dying, as an attempt to save the child for a state wishing to increase its population. They were not generally successful for mother or child.

Caesarean section or not, during the mediaeval period – for all women of every class – giving birth was incredibly perilous.

Breech presentations of the baby during birth often proved fatal for both mother and child. Labour could go on for days, and women could die of exhaustion.

Midwives with no formal training helped the mother-to-be during labour. They had a grim sideline – they were able to perform emergency baptisms on mothers and babies in danger of dying.

They had no training but did learn from years of experience … and the odd mistake or twenty.

New mothers might survive the birth, but Death was there to offer postnatal infections and complications. But the Grim Reaper wasn't entirely elitist; even Jane Seymour, the third wife of Henry VIII, died soon after giving birth to the future Edward VI in 1537.

2. Weather woes

Sunshine is delicious, rain is refreshing, wind braces us up, snow is exhilarating; there is really no such thing as bad weather, only different kinds of good weather.

John Ruskin (1819–1900), English writer

If John Ruskin had been a peasant, he would not have spouted such nonsense. Weather is one of the Grim Reaper's best friends and the peasant's greatest enemy.[8] ANY extreme is deadly.

From the 1300s through to the 1500s, the ice pack grew. By 1550, there had been an expansion of glaciers worldwide. This meant people faced the deadly effects of weather that was colder and wetter than average.

Superstitious mediaeval men and women would do anything to make sure the weather conditions stayed favourable. There were rituals for ploughing, sowing and the harvesting of crops, as well as special prayers, charms, church services and processions to guarantee good weather and fertility of crops and animals.

⇨ Saint Servais protected against frost.
⇨ Saint Elias took care of rain and droughts.
⇨ The Virgin Mary would protect against storms and lightning.
⇨ Saint Clement had the wind … so you wouldn't want to get on the wrong side of him.

Human actions could also affect the weather … no, not Global Warming in those days. SIN caused the weather to punish everyone.

---

8. Weather wasn't too kind to the dinosaurs either. Tyrannosaurus Rex became Tyrannosaurus Ex when the Triassic Met Office got it wrong. Michael Sawfish famously said, 'Earlier on today, apparently, a woman rang the Met Office and said she heard there was a meteorite on the way. Well, if you're watching, don't worry, there isn't.'

Murder, incest or simply family quarrels brought damnation in the shape of bad weather.

Witches and sorcerers could be responsible because they controlled the weather. In the infamous tract on witches – the *Malleus Maleficarum*, published in 1486 – they could fly in the air and conjure storms, hailstorms and gales, and bring down lightning that could kill people and animals.

That wouldn't be so bad if it was the sinning, murdering, incestuous humans. But it was anyone in the wrong place at the wrong time. So unfair, don't you think?

Deadly day

If you are feeling like death today, then the priest and physician at St Bartholomew's Hospital can tell your doctor if you will live or die. He will instruct your doctor …

> *Take the name of the patient and the name of the messenger sent to summon you. Take the name of the day on which the messenger first came to you. Join all the letters together and count them. If an even number results then the patient will not avoid death; if it is an odd number then he will recover.*
>
> John Mirfield (d.1407), physician

You can see the advantage to your doctor? If he knows you are going to die, he will decline to treat you. If he treats you and you end pushing up daisies then his reputation will suffer.[9]

The revolting peasants

> *One of the biggest reasons I left Elkton Hills School was because I was surrounded by phonies. That's all. They were coming in the goddam window.*
>
> J.D. Salinger (1919–2010), character Holden Caulfield,
> in *Catcher in the Rye*

Schools full of phonies? Surely not. Yet, every school student has been taught that the Black Death had benefits for the peasants who survived it …

---

9. Of course, you could always manipulate the messenger and the day to equal an odd number. The doctor will treat you. Just for fun you could then die in order to scupper his selfish plan and ruin his reputation.

Huge numbers of peasants died during Black Death and this meant that after the plague there was plentiful land, but landowners were short of peasants. This allowed the labourers to charge more.

'Interesting Facts about the Peasants' Revolt' website

Of course, some people have doubts about what they read on the internet. Unless it comes from a reputable site like the British Broadcasting Corporation ...

Since the Black Death, poor people had become increasingly angry that they were still serfs, usually farming the land and serving their king.

And history is made simple – black and white – for simple children like you and me ...

Feudal law during the time did not allow peasants to leave their village unless they had their lord's permission.

History for Kids website

And so, children like you and I grow and go through life believing the Black Death was 'a good thing' for peasants. But life is never that simple. The hold of the lords over the peasants was already growing weaker before the Black Death arrived.

The feudal pyramid was collapsing; those feudal duties had been increasingly allowed to lapse – or had been willingly excused against a modest money payment.

If lords tried to enforce their old rights, then they were as likely to succeed as today's monarch trying to impose the use of red telephone boxes instead of mobile phones. That ship had sailed, that horse had bolted, and that phone box was disconnected.

The great plague

When another virulent attack of the plague returned to London in 1666, the poor suffered death AND callousness on the part of the rich. A famous diarist was travelling by coach when his coachman fell sick. The great man hopped onto another cab smartish. He felt sorry for the coachman (of course) but was just as sorry for himself ...

It struck me very deep this afternoon going with a hackney coach from my Lord Treasurer's down Holborn, the coachman I found drove slower and slower, then at last stood still, and came down hardly able to stand. He told me that he was suddenly struck very sick, and almost blind, he could not see. So, I alighted and went into another coach with a sad heart for the poor man and trouble for myself lest he should have been struck with the plague, being at the end of town that I took him up; But God have mercy upon us all.

Samuel Pepys (1633–1703), naval administrator
and Member of Parliament

Accidents will happen

Accidents will happen in the best regulated families

John Dos Passos (1896–1970), American novelist

If the plague didn't get you then an accident could. There was no 999 service for the peasants who suffered an accident. Only pain, incapacity or death … you choose which is the worst of those three.

Coroners were introduced in 1194 and their records are revealing. Even simple accidents could prove fatal. There were many ways to die in the days of yore but here are a deadly dozen …

⇨ **Falls**   In November 1525, the criminal Thomas Sadd was incarcerated at Ramsey Abbey in Huntingdonshire. He attempted a night-time escape and managed to break out of the tower where he was being held. He fell from a height and broke his right leg. With no paramedics to administer antibiotics, he died six days later. Sadd, so sad. But other falls were so whacky, an unkind person may even laugh. In London, in January 1325, at around midnight …

John Toly rose naked from his bed and stood at a window 30 feet high to relieve himself towards the High Street. He accidentally fell headlong to the pavement, crushing his neck and other members, and thereupon died about cock-crow.[10]

---

10. He was waving his willie out of the window and died at 'cockcrow'. No pun intended by the chronicler … or was it?

⇨ **Animal bites** In 1544, Simon Reve, a tanner from Beccles in Suffolk, was passing through the courtyard of James Canne's house followed by his two mastiff dogs. His dogs quarrelled with Canne's greyhound, and ripped it apart. As Reve tried to break up the fight, he kicked one of his own mastiffs and the dog's tooth broke the skin on his sole. The wound was only one-eighth of an inch deep, but he died from it nine days later.[11] Unlikely killers were pigs; in Warwickshire in 1394, a pig bit Robert Baron on the left elbow, causing his immediate death. Previously, in London in May 1322, a sow wandered into a shop and mortally bit the head of one-month-old Johanna de Irlaunde, who had been left alone in her cradle.

⇨ **Crushing** A William Burre was an Essex labourer who died in 1589. Will had been holding up the front end of a cart while others mended it. It should have been a Jack. The cart moved, he fell over and a massive piece of timber fell on him. His back was crushed, and he died eleven months later. Now that's what you call back-breaking work.

⇨ **Drowning** Thomas Beettes was a butcher from Brentwood in Essex. He went out in 1589 for a few pints with friends. Later, replete with ale, he set off to walk home but was wearing a pair of slippers. The slippers slipped and he fell face-first into a full ditch and drowned. A lesson for us all – don't drink and drown.

⇨ **Scalding** Thomas Wright, a household servant from Milton in Dorset, was playing hand-tennis in 1581. An unusual sport for someone of the lower classes … and fatal in his case. His ball landed on top of a wall and he climbed up to gather it. He fell backwards into a brewing vat full of boiling wort – the liquid extracted from the mashing process during the brewing of beer. Badly scalded, he died that night. The wort was distributed to the poor people of the village. They probably drank his health. But a poor worker playing posh tennis? Served him right?

---

11. The coroner's jury decided the wound was not to blame so much as the astrological alignment of the stars. The 'Sign of the Foot' was dominant at that place at that time. There is no record of what happened to the dog.

⇨ **Domestic violence**

From time immemorial, husbands and wives have killed one another. But does Joan Clarice deserve sympathy for misguidedly trying to help her husband to a better life? John Clarice was lying in bed with his wife, Joan, at the hour of midnight. The coroner's report said …

Madness took possession of him, and Joan, thinking he was seized by Death, took a small scythe and cut his throat. She also took a bill-hook and struck him on the right side of the head so that his brain flowed forth and he immediately died.

Joan fled, and sought sanctuary in the local church. She later agreed to go into exile. Did she wash the pillow before she left? Brain flowing forth takes a bit of cleaning up.

⇨ **Knives**

Table knives weren't as safe and rounded as they are today. In the 1550s, 5-year-old Nicholas Braunche played with a knife he had picked up from a table. He tripped over the cradle of a younger child, fell and stabbed himself in the throat.

⇨ **Horses**

Horses were the transport and the tractors of the peasantry but just as dangerous as today's cars. Horses kick. Hard. But just once in a while, your sympathy is with the horse. Seven-year-old Robert Cranefold found a grey horse tied to a post and decided it would be fun to beat it with a twig. The victim didn't appreciate that sort of horseplay and kicked Robert in the head. The boy died. In 1581, a Shropshire servant, David Morrys, was equally deserving of his fate. He saw a mare locked up in the common pound after going astray. Dangerous Dave picked some stinging nettles with which to torture her. Lifting the mare's tail with his left hand, he put the nettles under her with his right. The mare was just as annoyed as he must have hoped. Sadly, she expressed her temper with a kick that caught him in the chest and killed him instantly.

⇨ **Workplace**

Some workplaces were dangerous before Health and Safety stepped in with its protective blanket of rules. Young Robert Alcocke was playing with other children in his father's blacksmith shop when a scythe and a large hammer fell on his head. And William Gregorys' father was fixing a cart in his barn when a wheel fell off and hit William on the head.[12]

⇨ **Sleeping**   Peasant children with uncomfortable homes (or no homes) could nod off to sleep in unlikely places ... and suffer. In the 1500s, George Nycolson slept by a lime kiln in Newcastle and was suffocated by smoke. Around the same time, Catherine Else fell asleep under a bridge at Marlow and was overcome by a wave when boats came through the lock.

⇨ **Sports**   The lords encouraged the peasants to maintain their martial skills in case they had to be conscripted in times of war. Archery was encouraged despite the obvious risks. In 1552, a child of 8 was killed in archery practice in Louth. Clearly the kid did not have an arrow escape. Shortly afterwards, a 10-year-old perished during a hammer-throwing contest in Corfe. Throwers of hammers – sledgehammers usually – always warned spectators of their imminent launches. But in 1591, weaver Robert Woode of Devon practised by throwing a hammer over the roof of a house. This bolt from the blue hammered innocent and unsuspecting passer-by Amicus Bykner.

⇨ **Pursuit**   People die in police pursuits regularly in modern times. But there is nothing new under the sun, as William Hutt, a chicken farmer from Northampton, reminds us. When the chicken business struggled, William turned to fowl play. In 1550, he tried forging coins. Law officers were sent to arrest him but he chicken-legged it. First, he leapt from a high wall, and crushed his left side on landing. He staggered to a millpond and jumped in, threatening to drown himself. The officers pulled him out and locked him in the town gaol. The chicken farmer made a clean breast of it and he confessed to forging nineteen or

---

12. In the USA, 'National Take Our Daughters and Sons to Work Day' is celebrated on the fourth Thursday in April each year. 'National Take Our Daughters and Sons to Work Day and Brain Them' is not.

twenty groats. But before he could be tried, he died from his injuries.

But the most ignominious death was maybe that of George Dunkyn, a Cambridge baker. In 1523, he returned from the tavern a little the worse for wear.[13] Unsurprisingly, he needed to relieve himself into the cesspit in the corner of his garden. The demon drink caused him to fall backwards into the pit. The coroner recorded that George was 'qweasomed' (suffocated) by the stink. What a way to go.

A Londoner, Roger the Raker, allowed his cesspit to fill to the floor. The floorboards rotted and he crashed through, and Roger the Raker, like George the baker, drowned.

Did you know …?

Cesspits fill up and have to be emptied. Not a chore most people relish. In 1347, two men were fined for attaching pipes to their sewage outlets and diverting it into the cellars of unfortunate neighbours. You have to hope the punishment included emptying what they had filled.

The pits

Our death is not an end if we can live on in our children and the younger generation. For they are us, our bodies are only wilted leaves on the tree of life.

Albert Einstein (1879–1955), German physicist

The rivers became polluted with human waste so those who could afford to moved uphill and upwind of the stench. They still needed to empty their toilets, of course. If a cesspit was a nuisance – in need of constant emptying – then a solution was to lay down a pipe from their mansion on the hill, down to the river.

Planning officers were not a problem for the rich. So, if the direct line from mansion to river ran through a graveyard, then the answer was obvious: move the bodies.

The Victorian music hall was the place to satirise such pretensions of the rich. How they must have enjoyed singing a song that claimed the ghosts

---

13. A curious phrase. 'The worse for beer' may be more accurate, don't you think?

of the unsettled skeletons would haunt the posh thrones and scare the bejeezus out of them.

> *Oh, they're moving father's grave to build a sewer*
> *They're moving it regardless of expense.*
> *They're moving dad's remains to lay down nine-inch drains*
> *To irrigate some rich bloke's residence.*
>
> *Now what's the use of having a religion?*
> *If when you're dead you cannot get some peace*
> *'Cause some society chap wants a pipeline for his trap*
> *And moves you from your place of rest and peace.*
>
> *Now father in his life was not a quitter*
> *And I'm sure he'll not be a quitter now.*
> *And in his winding sheet, he will haunt that privy seat*
> *And only let them sit when he'll allow.*[14]

Tragic. Even peasant lives should be allowed to end at their own convenience.

---

14. You may think the Victorian entertainers would substitute other words for the euphemisms 'trap' and 'sit'. I couldn't possibly comment.

Chapter 5

Housing

The strength of a nation derives from the integrity of the home.
                    Confucius (551–479 BC), Chinese philosopher

When Confucius was talking about the 'the home' he meant the integrity of the 'family' … not the 'house'. But the comfort of the house can decide the quality of your life.

Humans have been building houses for 1.8 million years, ever since some clever people built their first houses – in Tanzania. Home sweet home was a half-circle of lava blocks, probably roofed with branches. Not too comfortable but at least there's no rent to pay, no council tax and your neighbours don't park their BMW in the driveway next door to make you jealous.

Over those 1.8 million years, houses became more than a shelter for family and their domestic animals. They became a symbol of their status in society.

Lords built castles. They *looked* like defences against enemies. In truth, their main purpose was to hold the oppressed peasants in awe.

My name is Ozymandias, King of Kings;
Look on my Works, ye Mighty, and despair.
                    Percy Bysshe Shelley (1792–1822), English poet

The castle was raised on a mound so it could be seen from miles around. As the serfs laboured in the fields, they must have felt the windows of the castle looking down on them like the eyes of their lords.

At the other end of the main street would be the church – another symbol of a lord – a heavenly Lord. And, just in case they forgot their serf-duty to their heavenly oppressor, the church would have a tower to awe them.[1]

---

1. In some historic locations like Durham City, the cathedral towers are even higher than the castle across the road. It's almost as if the Church leaders were saying to the aristocracy, 'Our Lord's greater than your lord. Nurr-nurr.' What sort of god would be impressed by such one-upmanship … sorry, one-up-person-ship?

The peasants went home from their toil in the fields to houses that were not much advanced from their Tanzanian ancestors.

Cruck and muck

There is nothing more important than a good, safe, secure home.
Rosalynn Carter (b. 1927), American First Lady

Peasants lived in 'cruck' houses. The wooden frame had walls of woven branches – wattle. Of course, that lets the wind whistle through, so it needs to be plastered to keep out the draughts. The peasants used 'daub'.

This was a mixture of mud, straw and manure. The straw added insulation, but it was the manure that bound the mixture together and gave it strength, once it had dried.

All right, the disadvantage was the smell. But after you've plunged your hands into the droppings of your oxen or pigs, then you will smell just as bad and may not notice. And to keep those animals safe, they'd spend the night in a pen at the other end of your living room.[2] The animals would share their warmth ... their fleas, lice, bedbugs and other insects as well as their noise and their scents.

Walls that smell? 'Smell?' a mediaeval peasant would laugh. 'What smell?'

The daub mixture was left to dry in the sun and formed what was a strong building material. It was also quick and easy to repair ... no call-out charges for a cowboy builder. Just wait for your pig to empty its bowels then slap it on the cracks.

The peasant cruck houses had no chimneys, so you sat in a smoke-choked room. A fireplace was a luxury for the rich. Geoffrey Chaucer measured a woman's status by her chimney – or lack of it.

Full sooty was her bower
Geoffrey Chaucer (1343–1400), English poet,
in *The Nun's Priest's Tale*

Chaucer is also a source of information into the lifestyles of the peasant home. In his *The Reeve's Tale*, the two students staying overnight are given

---

2. Wild carnivores like wolves still roamed Britain in those days so it made sense to share your house with your precious livestock. And don't forget the human predators ready to nick a chick, snaffle a sow, cabbage your cow or misappropriate your mutton.

a made-up bed to share in the bedchamber; the room is shared with the miller and his wife (in one bed) and their daughter (who has her own bed). There is a baby in a cot.

At night the room would have been totally dark – candles cost too much money to use as a nightlight. If you needed a pee you'd have to get up, grope your way to the door – trying not to grope the miller's daughter on the way – and go outside to the toilet pit. Try not to fall in and drown. There would be no chamber pot for your convenience.

Did you know ...?

The droppings from domestic animals had more uses than simply keeping out draughts in wattle walls. If you suffer from baldness, then bake cow dung along with the soles of old shoes until they are dried. Grind them to a powder and mix with honey. Apply this paste to the bald head and cover with a cap for nine days.

Cruck castles

The idea of a house being a common person's domain was established as common law by the lawyer and politician Sir Edward Coke:

For a man's house is his castle, et domus sua cuique est tutissimum *refugium [and each man's home is his safest refuge].*
Sir Edward Coke, in The Institutes of the Laws of England (1628)

Sir Edward created an iconic image, but one that has caused a lot of trouble.

The 'Englishman's home is his castle' proverb was used in almost all of the articles about the court case of Tony Martin in 2000. Martin was convicted by jury trial of murder, after shooting and killing a 16-year-old who had broken into his house in Norfolk.

Prime Minister William Pitt the Elder (1708–1778) turned the house into a metaphorical castle ...

The poorest man may in his cottage bid defiance to all the forces of the crown. It may be frail – its roof may shake – the wind may blow through it – the storm may enter – the rain may enter – but the King of England cannot enter.

Old Pitt overlooked the fact that the king of England wouldn't *want* to enter. He'd send in some bully boys if the need arose. Do not quote Pitt's 'the King of England cannot enter' when the VAT inspector hammers at your door.

But those wattle and daub 'castles' of the mediaeval peasants were far from being physical castles. Like the house of a little piglet, a wolf could huff and puff and blow the house down.

Roxton ruin

Kill all the rich people. Break up their cars and apartments. Bring the revolution home, kill your parents, that's where it's really at.

Bill Ayers (b. 1944), American activist[3]

There was one horrific case in the Bedfordshire village of Roxton in the Middle Ages that demonstrated the problem with crap walls.

On 7 November 1269, the village of Roxton was rocked by the savage attack of a robber gang. It left five dead and three seriously injured.

A gang of armed thugs burst through the wattled walls of Ralph Bovetoun's house and robbed it as two girls staying there fled. The heavies carried off all of Ralph's possessions.

The people in the next house were not so lucky. Maude del Forde and Alice Pressade were in bed when the gang broke through. Maude was struck on the head with an axe. This was to stop her screams being heard, it was said. (Though you'd have thought breaking down poo-plastered partitions was fairly noisy?) Witnesses described seeing Maude's brains spilling out onto the pillow. Alice died later from the wounds they gave her.

When you're safe at home you wish you were having an adventure; when you're having an adventure, you wish you were safe at home.

Thornton Wilder (1897–1975), American author

John Cobbler's house was attacked on two sides with window shutters torn down and the door smashed in. The owner was taken outside and killed, along with his servant. His wife Azeline and daughter Agnes suffered axe

---

3. In 1997, Chicago awarded Mr Ayers its Citizen of the Year accolade for his work with schools. Draw your own conclusions about Chicago/USA. Just don't follow their lauded citizen's advice?

wounds to their heads and knife wounds to the chest and arms. Their other daughter managed to hide between a chest and a basket.

Azeline Cobbler survived long enough to tell the coroner that she recognised the wreckers. They were four glovers from Bedford. One of their jobs – when they weren't making mittens – was to collect church taxes for the monastery of Newnham. The tax-men-turned-axe-men had assessed the value of each villager's property. They knew exactly who to rob. (Not unlike Her Majesty's Revenue and Customs or Value Added Tax inspectors today, you might say.)

The Sheriff of Bedfordshire told worried villagers that these evil men would be caught and executed. It was probably the first ever police identity parade in history. The coroner took Azeline to the cells in Bedford so she could confirm the identities of the perpetrators.

Axed Azeline succeeded in doing this before she succumbed to her wounds and joined her husband in that great pig-poo palace in the sky.

If an Englishman's home is his castle, then a peasant's home was a sandcastle.

Did you know ...?

After Death and his scythe swished away almost half of the population with bubonic plagues, half a million houses were abandoned and fell into ruin between the 1350s and 1500. Records show that peasants were fined in increasing numbers for not keeping their houses in a good state of repair, or for demolishing buildings and taking the timber for use as firewood. It gives a whole new meaning to 'keep the home fires burning'.

An Irishman's home

> *The cup of Ireland's misery has been overflowing for centuries and is not yet half full.*

> Boyle Roche (1736–1807), Irish politician

The Middle Ages seem such a world away from our age it's tempting to think the peasant hovels died along with the end of the era. They didn't. In the age of the Georgians, with their fops and wigs, Handel and Wellington and carriages on cobbles, far from the gaslights of the cities, there was a darker world frozen in mediaeval misery.

In 1785, Britain's Attorney General John Fitzgibbon described the peasant life in Ireland:

The cottages of the Irish, which are called cabins, are the most miserable hovels that can well be conceived: they generally consist of only one room; mud kneaded with straw is the common material of the walls. These are rarely above 7ft high. They are about 2ft thick and have only a door which lets in the light instead of a window.

General John Fitzgibbon (1749–1802),
Lord Chancellor of Ireland (1789–1802)

At the same time, there were fine Dublin houses springing up like elegant mushrooms. Catholics – the overwhelming majority in Ireland – were harshly discriminated against even in housing. They were barred from holding property until 1793. The houses of Georgian Dublin were invariably owned by a small Church of Ireland Anglican elite.

The Catholic peasants could enjoy the elegant shelter of the Georgian houses when they skivvied below stairs as servants. If they couldn't get a job there, they could go to another fine building, designed by one of the Dublin star architects. It was Clifton House, located on Clifton Street in Belfast City. It was the Belfast Poor House for the destitute.

An escape from the mud cabins? Yes, but with a catch. The poorhouse children were the guinea pigs for the first trials of vaccinations in Ireland.

If the inoculations were to protect the young from disease, then why weren't they tried on the children of the rich, you have to wonder? But then …

We're all of us guinea pigs in the laboratory of God. Humanity is just a work in progress.

Tennessee Williams (1911–1983), American playwright

Dick the Kick

There is nothing like staying at home for real comfort.

Jane Austen (1775–1817), English writer

House-breaking didn't stop when houses were made of stone or brick. The famous highwayman Dick Turpin started his criminal career as a housebreaker. No, not a *burglar*. Literally, a house*breaker*.

Their technique was simple. The gang selected an isolated house where their intelligence said the owner had savings hidden away. One of the thugs kicked down a door and they then held the house owners at pistol point while their mates robbed them. Anything they couldn't carry away, they trashed and smashed.

In 1734, Turpin's Essex gang broke into a house and threatened to shoot the housewife they found there. She pointed out that if they shot her, she couldn't tell them where her savings were hidden. So, the leading thug threw logs on the fire till it was blazing then held the woman over it. The brave lady refused, but when her son came home, he told Turpin where her money was to save her further punishment.

There is nothing like 'staying at home for real comfort', eh, Ms Austen?

Terrible tenements

As villages grew into towns, the family home became a shared home. The detached house with its privacy became a privilege of the rich ... and they didn't even have to share it with farmyard animals, only lower-class servants.

The underclasses in the expanding towns were crammed into a small space and that space could be maximised by building upwards. Tenements were born.

> TENEMENT (especially in Scotland): a room or a set of rooms forming a separate residence within a house or block of flats.
>
> Dictionary

Sounds quite cosy ... and if you lived there you may be pleased. But the dictionary isn't satisfied with 'defining' the housing. It gave examples. And top of the example list is:

Various diseases all too often swept through entire city blocks of tenements.

Well, that's cheerful, isn't it? You live in your cosy box and some lexicographer in Oxford tells you it's a festering pit of disease.

Tenements were built (many in Glasgow) in the 1800s when there was an influx of workers to feed the hungry maws[4] of the factories during the Industrial Revolution.

---

4. Maws. A lovely word for the jaws or throat of a voracious animal. A much-underused word these days. Why don't we use it every day for a week and bring it back?

93

Those Scottish workers came from Ireland and from the Highlands, and were probably grateful for any sort of work and accommodation because – with neat historical serendipity – they were being thrown out of their old cottage homes (and their livelihoods) with the Highland clearances.

Always remembering …

We must not look at the past with the enormous condescension of posterity.

E.P. Thompson

… it does seem they were swapping their primitive crofts for the primitive tenements.

The clearances

By the end of the 1700s, the rich Highland landowners began throwing Highland smallholders off their poor farms. Not personally grabbing Highland families by the scruffs of their plaided necks, but using henchmen known as 'agents'. They had the backing of the law and the lawyers.

Make crime pay. Become a lawyer.

Will Rogers (1879–1935), American actor

Agents like Patrick Sellar seemed to relish the job more than most.

Sellar was the agent that Lord and Lady Sutherland employed to clear the highlander peasants off the land and turn their estates into sheep farms. Patrick Sellar stood trial in 1816 for the burning to death of an old woman who refused to vacate a house that was then torched. A jury of Sellar's peers – other local landowners who were probably bribed and bullied by Lord and Lady Sutherland – found him 'Not guilty'. Now there's a surprise.[5]

Even his employer, Lady Sutherland, called him …

Exceedingly greedy and harsh.

Lady Sutherland (1765–1839)

---

5. Sellar gave up his job as an agent but continued to make a good living. He kept sheep on the lands of the highlanders he'd evicted. His grandson, Walter Carruthers Sellar (1898 – 1951), made his fortune writing a comic history book, *1066 And All That*. WC's granddad's Highland clearances don't get a mention. Maybe they weren't funny enough?

Lady Sutherland was too, too understated. Compared to *her*, Sellar was a model of restraint and generosity. Between 1811 and 1820, about 15,000 crofters were forcibly removed from their Sutherlandshire homes, giving the lordly Sutherlands thousands of profitable sheep-farming acres. Lady Sutherland didn't see herself as treating her peasant farmers harshly. She saw the crofters as Highland cattle, bred to survive …

> *Scotch people are of happier constitution, and do not fatten like the larger breed of animals.*
>
> Lady Sutherland

The statue of the 1st Duke (Lord Sutherland) – nicknamed 'The Mannie' – stands near the village of Golspie in Sutherland. It is regularly vandalised to this day.[6]

When, in 1816, Sellar was accused of murdering the old woman who stayed in her house as it was burned down, his defence was brilliant: he explained it was the fault of the crofters themselves …

> *I see that I am accused of two serious crimes. Firstly, that I caused the death of a woman whose house was burned down, and secondly, that my sheep have eaten the people's corn.*
>
> *I am sure these things did not happen because I was cruel. If my sheep ate the people's corn because my shepherds were careless, the people should have complained to me and I would have done something about it.*
>
> Patrick Sellar (1780–1851), land factor, in a
> letter to the Duke of Sutherland

When, at the time of the arson, he was berated for setting the old woman's cottage on fire, he was a little less polite, saying …

> *Damn her, the old witch. She has lived too long. Let her burn.*

The argument that she had 'lived too long' was not one he used in his defence in court. The 'old witch' was 90 years old.

---

6. Sellar was buried in Elgin Cathedral – unlike his victims. Families have travelled from Canada to spit on his memorial.

Donald McLeod was one of the displaced persons. He wrote in his book *Gloomy Memories in the Highlands of Scotland* (pub. 1892):[7]

Little or no time was given for the removal of persons or property; the people striving to remove the sick and the helpless before the fire should reach them. The cries of the women and children, the roaring of the affrighted cattle, hunted at the same time by the yelling dogs of the shepherds amid the smoke and fire, altogether presented a scene that completely baffles description – it required to be seen to be believed.

I myself ascended a height about eleven o'clock in the evening, and counted two hundred and fifty blazing houses, many of the owners of which I personally knew, but whose present condition – whether in or out of the flames – I could not tell. The conflagration lasted six days, till the whole of the dwellings were reduced to ashes or smoking ruins.

Donald McLeod was persecuted by the aristocrats for his effrontery in exposing their savagery. His wife was driven incurably mad by the intimidation. Donald MacLeod and his family went to Canada, where he ended his days, an exile like his kin and friends.

As usual, when the peasants suffered, the very old and the very young bore the brunt … they were not 'the larger breed of animals' who could easily survive.

Some old men took to the woods, wandering about in a state approaching absolute insanity, and several of them, in this situation, lived only a few days, and several children did not long survive their sufferings.

Donald McLeod

After the croft houses had been destroyed, the families had to find new places to live.

A tenement in Glasgow must have seemed a haven.

'Mid pleasures and palaces, though we may roam,
Be it ever so humble, there's no place like home.

John Howard Payne (1791–1852), American actor,
poet and playwright, from the opera *Clari*

---

7. *'Gloomy Memories'* being the title in refutation of Mrs Harriet Beecher Stowe (author of *Uncle Tom's Cabin*) who wrote *Sunny Memories of Sutherlandshire*. Harriet had visited Scotland in 1851 and met the deadly Duchess of Sunny Sutherland. Maybe her view of the peasant population was coloured by that meeting? Just maybe.

The song was turned into a popular song in 1852 ... the year that the Highland and Island Emigration Society was formed. The policy appeared to be that if you can't persuade them to move to Glasgow, then ship them off to the wilds of Canada. Home, sweet home, indeed.

Patrick Sellar was especially keen to get the farmers off land at Rossal because he had rented it to put sheep on it himself. Many of the peasants are forgotten and their fates unrecorded. Yet Sellar is remembered ...

Did you know ...?

In a Glasgow pub there are two urinals in the gents' toilets. Take your pick – urinate on the one labelled Patrick Sellar or the one with Lord Sutherland's name imprinted on it. Tough choice.

Sellar is also remembered in a poem by a survivor of the clearances:

> *Loathsome Sellar, in your grave,*
> *Have you the pay you earned so well?*
> *The fire you used to burn the thatch,*
> *Does it now burn your beard in Hell?*

Grim Glasgow

When highlanders moved south to work in towns like Glasgow they needed somewhere to live. They were packed into the cheapest and gloomiest slum houses possible.

There were laws against overcrowding, even in the 1850s. A report said:

> *We started 'ticketing' houses. Police would raid them in the middle of the night and check they weren't overcrowded.*
>
> Victorian housing officer

The tenements varied in quality, so your quality of life depended on which tenement you got. In Dundee, in 1905, it depended which side of the road you lived on. The housing officer explained:

> Flat 1: This lucky family has a man, his wife and three children sharing two rooms. There are two toilets shared by twelve families in these flats.

Flat 2: This unlucky family, across the road, has a man, his wife, his son, two daughters and his wife's mother. They share a single room 3 metres by 4 metres. There are six toilets for the 429 people in this tenement block.

Even in the 'lucky' family, those two flushing toilets for twelve families may not sound like much, but in Dundee, forty years before, there were just *five* flushing toilets for the *whole* city of 92,000 people ... and three of those were in hotels. (Imagine the queues for the other two.)

So, the tenements were, as you'd imagine, a breeding ground for disease. Even the bubonic plague made a return visit there as late as August 1900. It has been described as 'relatively small', with only around thirty-six known cases and sixteen deaths. For the sixteen who died, it was *relatively* large.

It caused widespread panic. Rat-catchers were sent in – presumably the Pied Piper of Pollokshields was unavailable that week. There were desperate calls for a mass fumigation of the city's trams and ferries, and some called for the coins in people's pockets to be disinfected.

Of course, the poor old rats died to save the humans. But 2018 research found that secondary plague infections occurred between members of the same household. That puts the blame on body lice or human fleas.[8]

And in the twenty-first century, many of the surviving tenements have seen a surge in popularity among homebuyers. They've large rooms, high ceilings and historic details. The old tenement slums have now become some of the most valuable properties in the west end of Glasgow.

Did you know ...?

Restored tenements have their much older equivalents in the south of Britain. Some of the cruck houses are still standing 500 years after they were built from wattle and daub. The so-called 'cruck villages' in Buckinghamshire, Oxfordshire, Leicestershire and Warwickshire are so picturesque and quaint, they now sell for well in excess of three times the average national house price: not bad for a mediaeval peasant's poo palace.

---

8. Given the current fashion for government apologising for past wrongs, maybe the British government ought to issue a formal apology to the Glasgow rats?

One problem with this organic nature of the mediaeval house is that, while it holds heat well, it attracts vermin, which burrow into the walls and roof. In the modern cruck house survivors, the rats have moved out. The middle classes have moved in. Gentrification.

The dangerous slums

The inspectors of the Victorian housing conditions in many parts of Britain were shocked by what they found ...

> *Eleven persons had been living in this house for a long time with no other means than thieving. They were feeding themselves with a piece of roast beef, eggs, tea and some hot whisky. The rooms of the house were in the most filthy condition that can be imagined; it beggars description. I had occasion to search in one of the cupboards for stolen property and found there was a large deposit of human filth.*

And, like the mediaeval peasants, they often shared their living space with the animals they planned to eat ... though they probably didn't mention that to the animals.

> *There were four beds in that room, three people to a bed. Behind the beds was a hen roost with a deposit of hen filth. The smell from the room was overpowering.*

And the Victorian slums were seen as a breeding ground for crime.

> *Connecting the room with the one above was a trapdoor by which a person could escape from one room to another when pursued by the police.*

There were 'improvers' who wanted better conditions, but they started from the premise that the inhabitants of the slums were not 'the deserving poor', but only drunkards and thieves.

> *Field Lane, in Clerkenwell, was occupied entirely by receivers of stolen goods, which are openly spread out for sale.*
>
> Thomas Adolphus Trollope, in *What I Remember* (1887)

The police often excused their lack of action in these areas by claiming they were too dangerous to enter.

Charles Dickens, an insomniac, often walked these mean streets and had a better understanding.

> *I mean to take a great, London, back-slums kind of walk tonight, seeking adventures in knight errant style.*
>
> Charles Dickens, in a letter to friend

Yet the police were not convinced. The law said a citizen HAD to help a policeman in peril. Refusal could land you in jail. But the opposite happened, and the passers-by often helped criminals by warning them. As soon as they saw a policeman in the north of England, the cry was ...

> *Cheese my lads.*

In London, children chanted ...

> *I spy blue, I spy black,*
> *I spy a peeler in a shiny hat*

(Rhyming black and hat was NOT a crime ... though it ought to have been.)

Some children were taught by their parents to lie to the police. A man was accused of being drunk. His little daughter told the police ...

> *He couldn't have been drinking that afternoon. He was having a shave from 1 pm till 6 pm.*

For some reason, the officers of the law didn't believe this explanation and arrested the man anyway. The judge didn't believe the girl's perfectly plausible alibi. The man didn't get away with a close shave.

The perils of Plod

The (very real) dangers the police faced each day were a subject of satire ...

> *Our feelings we with difficulty smother*
> *When constabulary duty's to be done:*
> *Ah, take one consideration with another,*
> *A policeman's lot is not a happy one*
>
> W.S. Gilbert (1836–1911), English dramatist,
> librettist in *The Pirates of Penzance*

Hostility towards Robert Peel's finest wasn't confined to the neighbours of the criminals. The richer people were forced to pay the taxes that paid for the police wages.

Earl Waldegrave had a real hatred for the police. Waldegrave once paid a professional boxer to attack PC McKenzie in Piccadilly (London) while crowds of his friends watched. The boxer almost killed the policeman.

The rich even told their coachmen to lash out at policemen in the streets as they drove past. Some drove their coaches straight *at* the police officers.

Earl Waldegrave and a friend jumped on PC Wheatley and held him on the ground while his coach drove over him. PC Wheatley lived but was badly hurt. He never worked again.

The theory of law enforcement is beautifully symmetrical …

Public officers are the servants and agents of the people, to execute the laws which the people have made.
Grover Cleveland (1837–1908), American president

But when did practice ever follow theory? Victorian policemen worked ten hours a day and walked about 20 miles on duty. Nearly a marathon every day. They had no days off and only one week's holiday a year … and they didn't get paid when they were on holiday.

Birmingham had no police force in 1839. That year, riots started there, and the government sent for the London police. A hundred police eventually calmed the troubles. Then sixty policemen were sent back to London – and the rioters heard that only forty were left in Birmingham. The rioters drove the forty police into a yard and trapped them there while they ran through the town, burning and stealing. The army had to be sent in to free the police.

Arthur Conan Doyle's character Sherlock Holmes also portrayed the police as thick as custard.

'Come, Watson, come,' he cried. 'The game is afoot.'
Arthur Conan Doyle (1859–1930), Scottish writer,
in *The Return of Sherlock Holmes*

The 'game is afoot' meant something different to one London constable who remembered …

I found a wellington boot on the sea shore … with a man's foot inside it.

A policeman's lot – among the underclasses – was indeed an unhappy one.

Chapter 6

Religion

All religion, my friend, is simply evolved out of fraud, fear, greed, imagination, and poetry.

Edgar Allan Poe (1809–1849), American writer

And what, my friend, could be more poetic than going out and murdering someone who disagrees with your religion? Let's call that person a 'heretic'? Anyone who insults your religion, or your god/idol, is a 'blasphemer' and will be punished accordingly. Anyone who doesn't believe in ANY god is an atheist.

I'm an atheist … thank God. My church accepts all denominations – fivers, tenners, twenties.

Dave Allen (1937–2005), Irish comedian

And before organised religion there was superstition – a belief in fate and magic. The Celts in Britain had their druids with their 'nature' beliefs.

The geographer Strabo painted a dark image of human sacrifice, and the women were as culpable as the men …

Their wives, who would accompany them on their expeditions, were attended by priestesses who were seers; these priestesses would meet with the prisoners of war throughout the camp, and having first crowned them with wreaths would lead them to a brazen vessel of about twenty amphorae; and they had a raised platform which the priestess would mount, and then, bending over the kettle, would cut the throat of each prisoner after he had been lifted up; and from the blood that poured forth into the vessel some of the priestesses would draw a prophecy, while still others would split open the body and from an inspection of the entrails would utter a prophecy of victory for their own people; and during the battles they would beat on the hides that were stretched over the wicker-bodies of the wagons and in this way produce an unearthly noise.

Strabo (63 BC–AD 24), Greek geographer and historian

Naturally, the Romans wanted to stamp out this brutality. They had their own well-documented and organised pantheon. Gods like …

Cordea, the god of door hinges
The Penates, deities that will look after cupboards
Robigus, the god of mildew – that mouldy fungus that grows in damp places – and agricultural diseases like 'wheat rust' (that well-known cereal killer)
Sabazius, the god of barley and beer and generally any plants that are not a crop
Terminus, not the god of bus stations but the god of boundary markers
Furrina, a goddess of 'Other Things', but by 100 BC, no one could remember what she was goddess of.

The trouble is, the Romans KNEW their god system was right because poets like Virgil (70–19 BC) had written poems in which Jupiter declares …

I have given the Romans an empire without end.

Jupiter, top god in The Aeneid

So, anyone who *didn't* subscribe to the Roman gods was a heretic, and heresy has been punished with death throughout time. The druids were a top target.

Having anointed a human victim, they stab him with a small knife in the area above the diaphragm. When the man has collapsed from the wound, they interpret the future by observing the nature of his fall, the convulsion of his limbs, and especially from the pattern of his spurting blood. In this type of divination, the seers place great trust in an ancient tradition of observation.

Diodorus (90–30 BC), Greek historian

These were the religious killers that the Celtic peasants followed slavishly. Julius Caesar explained …

Throughout all of Gaul there are two classes of people who are treated with dignity and honour. The Druids and the warriors. This does not include the common people, who are little better than slaves and never have a voice in councils. Many of these align themselves with a patron voluntarily, whether because of debt or heavy tribute or out of fear of retribution by some other powerful person. Once they do this, they have given up all rights and are scarcely better than servants.

Julius Caesar

Most of us imagine the servile peasants were the product of the Norman Conquest and the feudal system. But the idea of a peasant 'class' goes back over a thousand years before William conquered. And what MADE the peasant class was the power of the priesthood.

Onward Christian soldier

I never saw, heard, nor read that the clergy were beloved in any nation where Christianity was the religion of the country. Nothing can render them popular, but some degree of persecution.

Jonathan Swift (1667–1745), Anglo-Irish
satirist and Dean of St Patrick's Cathedral, Dublin

No sooner had the Romans imposed their gods on the world than they changed their minds and turned Christian – they enforced the belief of one god with a son called Jesus.[1]

They sent Augustine to Britain as a missionary and he was no soft touch. The trouble was, when Augustine got to Britain, he found the Welsh Christians didn't worship the same way as the Roman Christians.

Augustine said the Welsh Christians should meet him and talk about the problem. They agreed to meet at an oak tree. Interesting choice of a 'sacred' oak tree – the remnants of druidic culture there, don't you think? Saint Dinas of Bangor Iscoed monastery set off to meet Augustine.

Before he left his monastery, a wise man told Dinas:

Let Augustine get to the meeting place first. He'll sit in his chair. Walk up to him. If he stands up to greet you, he is a humble man. Obey him. And if he sits on his backside, he is a proud man. Do not obey him.

Of course, Augustine didn't stand up. Augustine then told the monks, who were Britons, that they must go out and convert the heathen Saxons in England. The Welsh politely declined.

---

1. Jesus had been handed over to the Jerusalem judiciary by the *Roman* governor, Pontius Pilate. The Romans sent Jesus to his death, then ended up worshipping him … but the Romans liked to forget that and let the Jews take the blame.

Augustine flew into a very un-Christian rage and said God would destroy Dinas and his monastery. In fact, Gus didn't really trust God to do the job. He went to the Saxon King Ethelfrith (d. 616) and ordered him (in the name of God) to attack Chester. A messenger went from Chester to beg Ethelfrith for peace.

The messenger was sent back to Chester ... in a box ... chopped into little pieces.

The monks began to pray for the victory of the British against the Saxons. Of course, this upset their Saxon attacker. He asked who these praying monks were ...

> *When he was told that they were the priests of the Most High God, who had come to pray for the success of their countrymen, the Britons, he was very wroth, and, in the violence of his rage, rushed upon them, and murdered twelve-hundred of them in cold blood, without the least resistance on their part. Whilst this act of cruelty and barbarity was being perpetrated, Augustine was a spectator of the scene, and consenting to the massacre. Not more than fifty of them escaped. What the papists were then, they still remain – a vindictive people.*
>
> Theophilus Evans (1693–1767), Welsh clergyman and historian[2]

Did Ethelfrith really organise the massacre of the monks on Augustine's orders? The modern-day 'Papists' – Roman Catholics – refute Theo's rant against their church and their hero Augustine. 'Augustine was dead by AD601 when the alleged massacre took place,' they huff. 'He couldn't have watched it.'

Other historians point out that Augustine's signature can be seen on documents for years after the massacre.

What IS certain is that religious infighting among the Christians would lead to thousands of deaths down the centuries. And it would be the peasants who would suffer most as cannon fodder in the wars.

---

2. Not what you'd call a neutral reporter of history. Theo did tend to mix 'history' with 'legend'.

Having a Paddy

The druids didn't give up their powers over the peasants easily. Saint Patrick was sent to convert the Irish. The Irish druids came up with this nasty poem, attacking Saint Paddy …

> *Over the sea comes chopper-head*
> *Crazed-in-the-head*
> *His cloak has a hole for the head*
> *His stick is bent in the head.*
>
> *He will speak unholy words*
> *From a table in front of his house*
> *And all his people will answer:*
> *Amen. Amen.*

It's almost nonsense … and it's brilliant. You can practically hear the holy spluttering these words in their rage.

The Christian religion dominated Britain for centuries but, in the countryside where the peasants lived in closer contact with nature, the old pagan superstitions remained … and still do. Many ancient customs and beliefs linger. They go by the name of 'tradition' and 'heritage' these days. Townies roll up to watch the local yokels put on a show of dancing and drama, singing and supping ale.

The church elders knew this was anti-Christian and tried to discourage it. But when Henry VIII made himself head of the new Church of England, he had the power to enforce it.

May Day celebrations were banned by Henry and riots followed. Fourteen rioters were hanged, and Henry VIII is said to have pardoned a further 400 who had been sentenced to death.

The townies laugh at the simple peasant customs … then go home to enjoy their eminently 'sensible' Christmas, Halloween and Easter rituals.

Hello summer

The only liberty an inferior man really cherishes is the liberty to quit work, stretch out in the sun, and scratch himself.

H.L. Mencken

By 'inferior man' we can guess Menken means 'peasant'. So, if you like to take a holiday, lie in the sun and scratch yourself, then you are a peasant. Just be careful where you scratch yourself in public or you could be arrested and be an imprisoned peasant.

The peasants did enjoy their holy days. But May Day was always an odd pagan hangover … not the usual Christian holiday.[3]

In other countries it is Labour Day, and May Day was chosen as the date for International Workers' Day by the Socialists and Communists. They have huge parades in Russia to celebrate it. May Day is a wonderful day for running into the Moscow May Day Parade and singing (to the tune of *I've Got a Lovely Bunch of Coconuts*), 'I've got a lovely spray of Novichok'.

Come what May

What are the ancient practices that the peasants celebrated on May the First?

1. May Day was the day when country folk said 'Hello' to summer. Summer's reply is usually a north-westerly gale. The peasants went out into the woods and meadows to gather flowers and greenery and 'bring in the May'. Branches and blossom were used to decorate homes.
2. In the 1400s, Morris Dancers are first recorded. These bold, beribboned men blew the winter dust off their bells and danced on 1 May. These charming and simple, capering country folks have been sneered at, derided, ridiculed, scoffed and scorned ever since. Shameful.
3. Church-goers were not amused by the 'men attired in women's apparel' who led the Queen of the May into town. These cross-dressing men were known as May Marrions.
4. If Halloween is the festival of the dying year, then May Day is the festival of life. Still, like Halloween, it's a night when witches, fairies and ghosts wander the earth. The Fairy Queen rides out on a snow-white horse, looking for humans to lure away to Fairyland for seven years. Beware the seven-year witch.

---

3. Though some argue Christmas is not so much a Christian holiday as a Christian appropriation of the ancient Winter Solstice celebrations. A Pope called Julius decided on that date over 300 years after the birth. Wise Men argued for years that it was 16 or 20 May, 9, 19 or 20 April, 6 or 18 January, 29 March or 29 September. No one can say for certain.

5. On 30 April, young men and women went out into the woods and 'frolicked', returning on May Day morn. As Kipling put it delicately:

> *Oh, do not tell the Priest our plight, or he would call it a sin;*
> *But we have been out in the woods all night, a-conjuring Summer in.*

A Puritan was less delicate when he raged:

> *I have hearde of tenne maidens whiche went to set May, and nine of them came home with childe.*

Top marks for morality – big deduction for spelling.

Those lads and lasses came home on May Day with a tree (and nine babies, apparently).[4] They trimmed the branches to make a pole, painted it and decorated it with flowers. This was the maypole.

Maypoles

> *Line dancing is as sinful as any other type of dancing, with its sexual gestures and touching. It is an incitement to lust.*
>
> Ian Paisley (1926–2014), Irish politician and religious leader

1. Maypoles appeared in villages in the late 1300s. Couples joined hands and danced in a ring around a maypole. The custom probably started with those rotten Romans who carried a statue of their goddess Flora past a sacred, blossom-decked tree. The tradition spread across Europe from Italy. (Rather in the way the Black Death did.)
2. By the 1600s, maypole dancing was so much fun the Puritans banned it. That's their job really. The villagers dedicated May Day to Flora – 'A pagan goddess', the righteous killjoys raged.
3. By the 1700s, ribbons were tied to the top and woven into patterns.
4. The 1800s saw maypoles neglected and left to rot or used for firewood. (That's life: ash tree today, ashes tomorrow.)
5. Those romantic Victorians 'remembered' a past that never was, revived the old tradition and stuck up new maypoles – probably without

---

4. You just HAVE to wonder about maiden number 10. What was wrong with her that no lusty yokel wanted to impregnate her? Or did she pick a dud dude? There's a story in there somewhere.

planning permission. The people of Padstow in Cornwall still celebrate May Day with their Hobby Horse Carnival. The partying begins at dawn and goes on until sunset, by which time most of the pubs have run dry.

Queens of the May

1. The Queen of the May is elected each year to lead a May Day parade. She dressed in white to show 'purity'.
2. There is an old legend that says she was put to death at the end of the celebrations. A sort of sacrifice to the pagan gods of the summer.
3. But on May Day, the peasants DID drive their animals out to the summer pastures. At the end of the drive, they feasted on a male lamb killed that day. Lamb … chop, you might say. This could explain the 'sacrifice' myth. (There is no record of a May Queen being eaten … not even with some fava beans and a nice Chianti.)

Did you know …?

1. There are around seventy permanent maypoles in Britain. Wellow village in Nottinghamshire has the tallest at around 17 metres. They rot. The latest Wellow one was replaced in 2011 – with a steel pole. At a cost of £8,000, it was no steal.
2. The most famous maypole in England was erected on the first May Day of Charles II's reign in 1661. It was a towering 40 metres high (Nelson's column today is 52 metres). This maypole had to be floated up the Thames to stand in the Strand. It stayed there for almost fifty years.
3. Lewis Carol wrote *Alice in Wonderland* and enjoyed taking snaps of the book's inspiration, young Alice Liddell. In one of his most famous pictures she is posed as the Queen of the May. How sweet.
4. The 'Mayday' distress call has nothing to do with May Day. It's from the French cry for 'Help me' – *'m'aider'*. Be careful how you use it in the USA. A false distress call will earn you up to six years' imprisonment and/or a fine of up to $250,000. *M'aider?* You'll need it, matey.
5. On 1 May 1707, the Union with England Act was passed in the Parliament of Scotland, and two states became one. In 310 years, there has never been a single bid for independence by the English. It may one day. (May 1 day … geddit? Oh, please yourselves.)

4. Most queens were elected for their beauty, which is not PC these days.
5. But at Kidlington, the queen was chosen by her ability to catch and hold a lamb with her mouth, in a race against other young women. Much more PC ... but may upset vegetarians.

The holidays

There were no Bank Holidays for peasants but there were enough Saints' and Holy Days to allow some relief from the drudgery. Then there was Christmas.

Cruel at Christmas

Christmas in Tudor times was an excuse to kill the fatted calf ... or, more usually, a pig. On Christmas Eve 1567, Jane Typtott of Suffolk grabbed the pig they'd been fattening up all year. She lifted the animal onto a bench to slaughter it. The pig, however, was lacking in the Christmas spirit. It struggled. We aren't fluent enough in pig-psychology to know if it was afraid of heights or the butcher's knife. But as it writhed (and squealed, no doubt) it knocked Jane over. As she fell, she stabbed herself in the right leg with her knife and died soon afterwards.

The coroner did not record the fate of the pig, but we can guess it would be a crackling Christmas in that household.

Potted Palm Sunday

On Palm Sunday, the boys of Chippenham in Wiltshire climbed onto the church roof to throw small cakes to the crowd below. What a charming old custom, you say? In 1507, Francis Gore and Nicholas Hulkebere were pious lads, on the path by the church in the procession. As the virtuous villagers scrambled for the cakes, two of the cap stones from the roof were knocked off by the cake-chuckers. They crushed Francis and Nicholas, and before they knew it, they were singing in the heavenly choir.

And when the peasants weren't holidaying, they were working to fill their stomachs ...

Chapter 7

Food

Poison is in everything, and no thing is without poison. The dosage makes it either a poison or a remedy.

Paracelsus (1493–1541), Swiss physician,
alchemist and astrologer

Food poisoning

The peasant house would have no running water and, of course, no toilet. The toilet would have been a bucket, which would have been emptied into the nearest stream or river each morning.

Peasants would need water for cooking, washing and drinking. The water usually came from the same source, and you can imagine the consequences. A village with a well was much safer *unless* someone fell down it, of course.

Did you know …?

In 1389, at Coventry, Johanna Appulton was drawing water from a well when she fell in. A second servant ran to help, but she fell in too. This was overheard by a third person who also went to their rescue … and, you guessed it … he too fell in. All three drowned.

Well, well, well.

Water was collected in wooden or leather buckets. Villagers who had access to a well could simply wind up their water from the well itself.[1]

And polluted water wasn't the only threat. Storing food over the winter could give you a type of food poisoning. Ergotism.

---

1. If you are ever tempted to replicate the simple peasant life, then go ahead. Even if you have fresh well water, don't use the same bucket for water during the day and toilet waste at night. Just don't.

Ergot

Ergotism is the name for an illness caused by plant material containing ergot alkaloid, such as contaminated grain.

The Hospital Brothers of St Anthony, an order of monks established in 1095, specialised in treating ergotism victims so the common name for ergotism is 'St Anthony's Fire'.

The fire referred to the intense burning sensations in the limbs, which was one of the symptoms.

One type of ergotism gives the sufferer muscle spasms and fever; the victims may appear dazed, be unable to speak or have other forms of paralysis or tremors, become manic and suffer from hallucinations and other distorted perceptions.

The second type of ergotism is marked by violent burning, shooting pain from bad circulation to the fingers and toes. This could sometimes lead to gangrene and loss of limbs.

A 1355 chronicler was able to describe the frightening symptoms without understanding the cause:

People went out of their minds and behaved like madmen in fields and towns. Some fled into woods as if they were mad beasts shunning the presence of humans. Some ran into fields where it was exceeding difficult to catch them. They wounded themselves with knives or tore with their teeth at those who tried to capture them. Many were led into church and left there, bound, until they received some relief from God. It was a great sorrow to behold their suffering.

Knighton's Chronicle (1355)

The chronicler's best explanation for the erratic behaviour was that the sufferers were infested with evil spirits.

Famine

Dirty water was better than no water and dodgy food was better than no food. But sometimes, the no-food option was all that was on the menu.

False words are not only evil in themselves, but they infect the soul with evil.

Socrates

Words are powered by batteries. Over time they run down and have to be replaced.

Take the word 'hunger'. It is now called 'food deficit'. If a lot of people are hungry at the same time, it's not a 'famine' these days, it's a 'food crisis'. And peasants knew all about those.

Modern estimates suggest that Britain suffered from ninety-five food crises during the Middle Ages. Some of the worst included the 1235 famine, when some 20,000 Londoners died of starvation and many resorted to eating tree bark for survival.

Then came 1306 and the Great Frost. Four months of winter snow and ice made life a misery for the poor …

There was such a chill and such masses of ice on the Thames (and everywhere else) that the poor were overcome by excessive cold. The river froze so solidly, bonfires could be lit on it.

Chroniques de London

There were benefits in the freeze. Fish died in the ponds, so the peasants had frozen fish fingers to hand. Cattle froze in the fields and birds fell to earth. From sky to pie in no time. But worse was to come …

1315–1317, The Great Famine[2]

Abnormally heavy rains and cold led to bad harvests. People often resorted to killing their horses and farm animals for food – and to save feeding them.

They ate their seed corn, so they'd struggle the following year to grow more. It was another ten years before seed stocks were replenished enough to return to pre-famine levels.

Peasants resorted to gathering wild edible roots, plants, grasses, nuts and bark in the forests, just like their Stone Age forebears.

Some of the elderly refused to eat as a way to allow the younger population to survive. Malnutrition lowered peasant resistance to diseases such as pneumonia, bronchitis and tuberculosis, and led to mass deaths. Life expectancy was just 29 years and 10–25 per cent of

---

2. Some argue that the impact went on for far longer than two or three years, so it could be 'The Great Famine of 1315–1322'. You pays your money …

populations in some towns died. In England alone, maybe 500,000 died in 1315–16.

The price of corn in Norfolk quadrupled. Many peasants resorted to banditry to live.

Cannibalism and infanticide increased. Children were abandoned to fend for themselves ... a folk memory recorded in tales like *Hansel and Gretel*.

Edward II of England was travelling through St Albans, and even he failed to get any food on 10 August 1315 because his servants could find no bread.

The famines weakened the feudal system as the peasants were spread more thinly – literally, if you were a cannibal making peasant meat-paste. The Black Death of thirty years later reduced the population still further and the survivors had more food to go around. This was no consolation to the dead ones.

Church attendances declined as people discovered no amount of praying put food in their bellies and they blamed God for the foul weather. The priesthood, they claimed, was corrupt, and the famine was God's punishment.

The church retaliated and told the peasants it was THEIR fault that God sent the bad weather ...

> *When God saw that the world was so over proud,*
> *He sent a dearth on earth and made it full hard.*
> *A bushel of wheat was at four shillings or more,*
> *Of which men might have had a quarter before ...*
> *And then they turned pale who had laughed so loud,*
> *And they became all docile who before were so proud.*
> *A man's heart might bleed for to hear the cry*
> *Of poor men who called out, 'Alas. For hunger I die ...'*
>
> Poem on the Evil Times of Edward II,
> Middle English poem (1321)

Another phase of the Little Ice Age brought famine back to Europe in the 1590s. Many peasants had become paid labourers by this time, with no land of their own – no seed corn or draught animals to tide them over. Their paltry wages had to cope with rising prices.

Fat friends

In any society there are always exceptions to the rule. A peasant who entered the household of a lord could avoid days of hunger. In the 1460s, Lord Strange of Lancashire had a letter written to his rich relative, recommending a 'true servant' Robert for an easy, indoor job. Why? Because …

> *Robert my servant is a true servant to me, nevertheless he is large to ride and over-weighty for my horse.*

A fat peasant? You have to feel sorry for the horse.

Irish woe

> *Being Irish, he had an abiding sense of tragedy, which sustained him through temporary periods of joy.*
>
> William Butler Yeats (1865–1939), Irish poet

The sufferings of the Irish Famine in 1845 – following the failure of the potato crop – are remembered. But Ireland's long history of hunger shouldn't be forgotten:

⇨ Stories like *Hansel and Gretel* – a wood dweller luring children into their homes to be eaten – may have been based on fact. During an Irish famine an old lady who lived near Newry in the north-east of Ireland was said to be the fiend in the forest.

⇨ In Tudor times, an unsympathetic English poet blamed the Irish rebels for their own misery. He believed that 'Ireland is a diseased portion of the State, it must first be cured and reformed, before it could be in a position to appreciate the good sound laws and blessings of the nation.' A scorched earth policy would eradicate the rebels, he advocated. Famine, then, was a useful weapon against revolting peasants and he witnessed it at work …

> *Out of every corner of the valleys they came creeping forth upon their hands and knees, for their legs would not carry them. They looked like Death in human form. They spoke like ghosts crying out of their graves. They ate dead and rotting animals, happy when they could find them. They soon turned to eating one another and did not mind scraping open graves to get at the carcasses. If they found a patch of*

watercress or shamrocks they flocked around it as if they were at a feast. In the war there were not many who died by the sword, but many who died of famine, which they brought on themselves.

Edmund Spenser (1553–1599), English poet

⇨ In 1583, Sir Philip Sydney – a slightly less brutal Brit poet – visited Ulster and spent the night in a peasant's home. He wrote:

Half a dozen children, almost naked, were sleeping on a little straw with a pig, a dog, a cat, two chickens and a duck. The poor woman spread a mat on a chest, the only piece of furniture in the house and invited me to lie there. The animals greeted the first ray of the sun with their cries and began to look for something to eat. I got up very soon for fear of being devoured.

Philip Sydney (1554–1586), English poet

⇨ In the 1602 famine there were stories of cannibalism. One tale told of a family where the mother died. The girl made some stew for her brother. He ate it before he went off to bury his mother. When he returned an hour later, he shook his head and said, 'When I buried her, I noticed a strange thing. Mother had one leg missing. Where can it have gone?'
And his sister smiled and said nothing. She just licked her lips.

Solving the problem

The most brilliant satire of all time was A Modest Proposal *by Jonathan Swift. You'll notice how everything got straightened out in Ireland within days of that coming out.*

P.J. O'Rourke (b.1947), American satirist

In the 1720s, there was no social media to spread news of the plight of the Irish peasants among the people with wealth enough to help them. But there was a powerful weapon: satire.

A Modest Proposal For preventing the Children of Poor People From being a Burthen to Their Parents or Country, and For making them Beneficial to the Publick

Title of pamphlet by Jonathan Swift

Across the country, poor children, mainly Catholics, were living in squalor because their families were too poor to keep them fed and clothed. Swift proposed an answer that was as ingenious as it was simple.

He began by bemoaning the state of the peasants …

It is a melancholy Object to those who walk through this great Town [Dublin], or travel in the Country; when they see the Streets, the Roads, and Cabin-doors crowded with Beggars of the Female Sex, followed by three, four, or six Children, all in Rags, and importuning every Passenger for an Alms.

His proposal was to fatten up those undernourished children, butcher them and feed them to Ireland's rich landowners. Children of the poor could be sold into a meat market at the age of one, he argued. This would:

⇨ combat overpopulation
⇨ spare families the cost of child-rearing
⇨ provide them with a little extra income
⇨ the upper classes, at the same time, would enjoy a healthier diet and add to the economic well-being of the nation
⇨ and husbands would appreciate their cash-cow wives more.

Swift added recipes and suggested talented chefs could add their own.

A young healthy child well nursed, is, at a year old, a most delicious nourishing and wholesome food, whether Stewed, Roasted, Baked, or Boiled; and I make no doubt that it will equally serve in a Fricassee or a Ragout

Sorted. Except, of course, this was Swift's satire on the heartless indifference of society to the poor. Many (humourless) readers were outraged; he was branded everything from a savage cannibal to an insane maniac. The outraged included the queen.

Others, like Lord Bathurst (father of nine), got the joke and responded in kind …

I did immediately propose it to Lady Bathurst, as your advice, particularly for her last boy, which was born the plumpest, finest thing, that could be seen; but she fell in a passion, and bid me send you word, that she would not follow your direction, but that she would breed him up to be a parson, and he should live upon the fat of the land; or a lawyer, and then, instead of being eaten himself, he should devour others.

The essay was a commercial success, but Swift was deeply disturbed at the nation's response – or lack of the response he'd hoped for. He had imagined the Irish people would take action against the British government and aid the poor. Instead, the situation worsened on all fronts.

The joke fell flat.

Tea for ewe

When a man's stomach is full it makes no difference whether he is rich or poor.

Euripides

No difference? Not quite true. The rich have their stomachs filled more frequently, more completely and more hygienically than the poor.

In the 1720s, tea was a luxury that the rich could afford. The poor were driven to buying smuggled tea. The smugglers were greedy entrepreneurs who realised they could maximise their profits – like today's drug dealers – by adulterating their product with a cheaper substance. If you want to make a fast buck, then here is how an English tea smuggler advised his retailers to do it:

⇨ Gather leaves from ash and elder trees.
⇨ Spread them to dry and wither for a week.
⇨ Soak sheep's dung in a bucket of water for a few days till the water turns green.
⇨ Steep the withered leaves in the water till they are dyed green and have a 'herbal' flavour.
⇨ Place them in an oven to crisp.
⇨ Sift and send to a local expert for blending with the genuine imported tea.

If you want to emulate the recipe today you could market it as having 'all-natural ingredients'.

The idea of drinking a brew made from sheep droppings may disgust you, but those who didn't *know* the provenance of their green tea may have enjoyed their refreshing cup.

Georgian Class

One of Dean Swift's rivals in the early Georgian era was Daniel Defoe (1660–1731). In 1709, he had written a simplified analysis of British society. The peasants were still at the bottom …

1. *The great, who live profusely*
2. *The rich, who live plentifully*
3. *The middle sort, who live well*
4. *The working trades, who labour hard, but feel no want*
5. *The country people, farmers, &c, who fare indifferently*
6. *The poor, that fare hard*
7. *The miserable, that really pinch and suffer want.*

Defoe had simplified the classes of society in Georgian Britain to seven. But it was bleak if you inhabited that seventh circle of Hell …

⇨ A Georgian family were found dead in a barn and an autopsy showed their stomachs had nothing in them except grass. In a later Victorian case, the family had raw turnip in their dissected stomachs … and this was not the time of the Irish Famine.

⇨ In 1757, a mother and nine children in Buckinghamshire went several days without food. The mother found some money and bought the heart, liver and lungs of a calf to make a meal. Then she set off to gather fire wood to cook the offal. By the time she's returned, the children had eaten every scrap, gullet and all.

⇨ The same year, a mother and two children in Cumberland had no bread and tried to survive on horse bran. They were all found dead one morning and the children had straw in their mouths.

At the other end of Defoe's scale …

Class 1 'The Great – who live profusely' (with a lot to spare)
The Duke of Chandos had his own orchestra of twenty-seven musicians while Sir Robert Walpole spent £1,500 a year on wine (£90,000 today) and £1 every night on candles (the Miserable could buy food, drink, fuel and shelter for five weeks for that £1).

But even at the lower end there were some surprisingly successful survivors …

Class 6 'The Poor - whose lives are hard'

A family of seven in Derbyshire lived in a cave. The father was a lead miner and had been born in the cave, so had his five children. The cave was divided into three rooms by curtains and a hole had been dug through the roof to make a chimney. A pig and its piglets ran around the door. The miner earned about £6 a year and his wife would wash the lead ore and earn another £4 a year.

Defoe wrote:

> *Things inside did not look as miserable as I'd expected. Everything was clean and neat, and they seemed to live very pleasantly. The children looked plump and healthy, the woman was tall, clean and attractive.*
>
> Daniel Defoe

When Defoe gave her some money she almost fainted with happiness.

Class 5 'The Country People – who manage indifferently' (not too well)

The days of the peasant families with their own strips of land were finished by Georgian times. A writer said the main problem was the country people owned nothing. They used to keep a cow and a pony, a goose and a pig on the 'common' land. They'd have the odd wild rabbit, nuts and berries. But from Tudor times onwards, the common land was fenced off and sold to the richer farmers. The poor workers couldn't afford a large farm and there weren't any small ones. What was the point in working? A writer said:

> *Go to an ale house in the country and what will you find? It is full of men who could be working. They ask, 'If I work hard will I be allowed to build my own cottage? No. If I stay sober will I have land for a cow? No. If I save up can I get half an acre for potatoes? No. All you are offering me is the workhouse. Bring me another pot of ale.'*

Peasant life in the pre-industrial country hadn't been fresh air and roses. You worked when the farmer wanted you – harvest or sowing times – and you went hungry the rest of the year. Then came the Industrial Revolution and machines began to reduce the need for labourers. The wars with France in the late 1700s and early 1800s increased the demand for food production for a while. Then it was back to the hunger days.

Foul food

Once, during Prohibition, I was forced to live for days on nothing but food and water.

W.C. Fields (1880–1946), American comedian

Agricultural peasants' revolts weren't just a product of the miserable Middle Ages. In 1830, the Swing Riots – mainly protests over mechanised threshing – broke out in Kent and soon spread across the country. Rioters were hanged, transported or jailed.

A new Poor Law improved food, shelter and living conditions in the workhouses. The Poor Law of 1832 had two guiding principles:

1. Relief for the able-bodied should only be available in the workhouse.
2. The pauper should have to enter a workhouse with conditions *worse* than those of the poorest 'free' labourer outside of the workhouse.

Many were pits of misery and despair. Writers railed against the system. Charles Dickens did more than anyone to perpetuate the legend of harsh workhouses and their food. One of the most famous scenes in literature describe a hungry boy's plea for seconds:

The evening arrived; the boys took their places. The master, in his cook's uniform, stationed himself at the copper; his pauper assistants ranged themselves behind him; the gruel was served out; and a long grace was said over the short commons. The gruel disappeared; the boys whispered each other, and winked at Oliver, while his next neighbours nudged him. Child as he was, he was desperate with hunger, and reckless with misery. He rose from the table; and advancing to the master, basin and spoon in hand, said, somewhat alarmed at his own temerity:
'Please, sir, I want some more.'

Charles Dickens, in *Oliver Twist*

Then the popular theatrical monologue *Christmas Day in the Workhouse* told a fictional tale of an old man whose wife was too proud to enter the workhouse. The parish refused 'relief', so she died. The old man went back to rage against the workhouse governors. It is a wonderful parody on the Victorian taste for mawkish sentimentality, yet it still has the power to evoke the age as the old man describes his wife's fate …

Then she rose to her feet and trembled, and fell on the rags and moaned,
And, 'Give me a crust, I'm famished… for the love of God!' she groaned.
I rushed from the room like a madman and flew to the workhouse gate,
Crying, 'Food for a dying woman!' and the answer came, 'Too late.'
They drove me away with curses; then I fought with a dog in the street
And tore from the mongrel's clutches a crust he was trying to eat.

George R. Sims (1847–1922), English satirist

It was meant as satire but of the blackest kind. It was an attack on the rich who gave charitably to the poor, but only in the framework of rigid rules and with a lot of condescension.

Yes, there in a land of plenty, lay a loving woman dead.
Cruelly starved and murdered for a loaf of the parish bread;
At yonder gate, last Christmas, I craved for a human life,
You, who would feed us paupers, what of my murdered wife?
There, get ye gone to your dinners, don't mind me in the least,
Think of the happy paupers eating your Christmas feast
And when you recount their blessings in your parochial way,
Say what you did for me too… only last Christmas Day.

The poem was meant as an entertaining music hall joke at the expense of the straight-faced, straight-laced (and very bad) poets of the time. Yet George Sims was astounded to discover – late in life – that his humour was treated as a serious piece of peasant propaganda. He said :

Christmas Day in the Workhouse *was for a time vigorously denounced as a mischievous attempt to set the paupers against their betters, but when a well-known social reformer died recently I read in several papers that he always declared that it was reading* Christmas Day in the Workhouse *which started him on his ceaseless campaign for old age pensions, a campaign which he lived to see crowned with victory.*

George R. Sims

Writers like Dickens have left a lot of us with the impression that the poor survived on a diet of gruel (thin porridge) and water. But Oliver Twist's experience in the workhouse was five-star luxury hotel compared to some realities of Dickens's day.

The Andover scandal

Bone crushing was a common occupation for paupers. They were given the bones of horses, dogs and other animals (and there were rumours that some came from local graveyards). Paupers crushed the bones to make fertiliser for local farms. But the Andover Workhouse paupers were so hungry that they scrambled for the rotting bones when they were unloaded.

Boys as young as 8 worked in pairs to operate the heavy hammers (or 'rammers') to break open the bones.

An interview with a workhouse inmate was recorded verbatim:

Mr Wakley: During the time you were so employed, did you ever see any of the men gnaw anything or eat anything from those bones?
Charles Lewis: I have seen them eat marrow out of the bones.
Mr W: Did they state why they did it?
CL: I really believe they were very hungry.
Mr W: Did you yourself feel extremely hungry at that time?
CL: I did, but my stomach would not take it.
Mr W: Did you see any of the men gnaw the meat from the bones?
CL: Yes.
Mr W: Did they use to steal the bones and hide them away?
CL: Yes.
Mr W: Have you seen them have a scramble and quarrel amongst the bones?
CL: I do not know that I have seen them scramble, but I have seen them hide them.
Mr W: And when a fresh set of bones came in, did they keep a sharp look-out for the best?
CL: Yes.
Mr W: Was that a regular thing?
CL: While I was there.

In 1845, the Master of the Andover Workhouse was one Colin McDougal, a Waterloo veteran with a taste for sadism. His wife, Mary Ann, was described as 'a violent lady', and they ran the institution like a penal colony. He was a drunkard too and, as a sideline, attempted to seduce the young women in his care. To save money he once forced a poor woman to carry her own baby in its coffin to the cemetery for burial.

McDougal was paid a fixed sum to feed each pauper. Naturally, if he fed them less, he could pocket the difference in cash. So, the inmates starved. They even ate with their fingers because the Master and Mistress had sold the cutlery.

During the bone crushing, flying shards of bone often stabbed the inmates in the face or body and the hammers blistered their hands. Colin and Mary Ann McDougal found it a profitable trade. They bought bones at 17 shillings a ton and sold the bone dust at 24 shillings a ton.

At last, a charity governor of the workhouse found out what was going on. He raised his concerns with his MP and seventeen months later, reforms were implemented. (The wheels of Parliament grind exceeding slow.)

Amazingly, some paupers were resigned to their lot and did not complain to the inspectors. At the enquiry, 61-year-old Samuel Green described what happened when fresh bones arrived at the Andover Workhouse:

I like the fresh bones – I never touched one that was a little high; the marrow was as good as the meat. It was all covered over by bone; that was when they were fresh and good. Sometimes I have had one that was stale and stunk and I eat it even then. I eat it when it was stale and stinking because I was hungered, I suppose. You see we only had bread and gruel for breakfast, and as there was no bread allowed on meat days for dinner, we saved our bread from breakfast, and then, having had only gruel for breakfast, we were hungry before dinner-time. To satisfy our hunger a little, because a pint and a half of gruel is not much for a man's breakfast, we eat the stale and stinking meat. The allowance of potatoes at dinner on meat days is half a pound, but we used to get nearly a pound, seven or eight middling sized potatoes. The food we got in the workhouse was very good; I could not wish better, all I wanted was a little more. I have seen a man named Reeves eat horse-flesh off the bones.

As a result of the report, the McDougals were found to be unfit to hold their posts as Master and Matron of the Workhouse. In McDougal's place they appointed a new master, who was a former prison officer. If the inmates had frying pans and fires, they'd have found they'd jumped out of the former into the latter. The new master was dismissed within three years for taking liberties with female inmates.

The price the poor paid for food and shelter was humiliation. The price they paid for what we take for granted.

Many a man curses the rain that falls upon his head and knows not that it brings abundance to drive away the hunger.

Saint Basil (330–379), Greek monk

The peasants who had blood sugar levels to spare could always indulge in sport to expend their energy …

Chapter 8

Sport

Serious sport has nothing to do with fair play. It is bound up with hatred, jealousy, boastfulness, disregard of all rules and sadistic pleasure in witnessing violence. In other words, it is war minus the shooting.

George Orwell (1903–1950), British author

Football foul

Britain's top national sport is football … or 'soccer', if you speak English with a transatlantic accent but can't actually play the game.

There is the unsubstantiated statement that …

Football is a gentleman's game played by hooligans, and rugby is a hooligans' game played by gentlemen.

Winston Churchill (1874–1965), British politician …
but probably apocryphal

You can see the flaw in the logic. The speaker is trying to say that if someone is a 'gentleman' then he cannot also be a hooligan. Given the gentlemanly preoccupations with huntin', shootin' and fishin' – and generally killing unarmed animals – then there are millions of foxes, pheasants and trout who would argue gentlemen are far from gentle.[1]

Camp ball – Middle Ages

If you don't believe you can win, there is no point in getting out of bed at the end of the day.

Neville Southall (b 1958), Welsh international footballer

---

1. At least they WOULD argue that if they were not (a) dumb animals and (b) dead.

A game that was the ancestor of football probably started among the peasants … but that doesn't make them hooligans.

The mediaeval game of camp ball was similar to football with hands. You grabbed the ball and tried to get it into your opponent's goal a few dozen yards or a couple of miles apart. Running, throwing, passing or kicking the ball were all acceptable.

There were any number on each side and hardly any rules. The trouble was there were no football strips – players wore their normal clothes … including the knives they kept handy for work or dinner.

In Newcastle upon Tyne in 1280, Henry de Ellington ran into David le Keu. David was wearing a knife at his belt, the knife stabbed Henry in the gut and he died. Deadly David didn't get a red card[2] but hacked Henry probably got a very red shirt.

Everyone carried a knife at their belt for mealtimes. Many mediaeval players were injured falling on their own knives. That, of course, could give someone an excuse to carve up an enemy and *allege* that it was self-inflicted. But as a player and manager said …

> *Allegations are all very well, but I would like to know who these alligators are.*
>
> Ron Saunders (b. 1932), football player and manager

Let's hope he got a snappy answer.

In 1410, Henry IV's government imposed a fine of 20 shillings and six days' imprisonment on those caught playing football. Some fans believe this law should be brought back for certain players in their team.

Scotland scorcher

> *If the men want to practise a sport then they should try something useful, like archery.*
>
> James II of Scotland (1430–1460)

Miserable James II of Scotland banned football and golf in 1457. The only balls he approved of were cannonballs.

James II became a great fan of those new cannon things. He brought them from over in Flanders. He saw them as mean machines that would

---

2. After all, it was an accident, ref, not a professional foul.

help him attack English Castles. His plan was to knock all their northern castles down while the English were fighting each other in those Wars of the Roses.

Jim marched on Roxburgh with his favourite cannon, a monster he called 'The Lion'. He raised a hand and cried, 'Fire'. The gunner lit the fuse. The fuse burned down. The gunpowder exploded … and blew the Lion apart. A great lump of metal sliced the king's leg off – or off-side if you enjoy a footballing metaphor. He was soon dead.

As a later Scotland football team boss said …

> *He's got the legs of a salmon.*
> Craig Brown (b. 1940), Scottish football manager

Another entertaining – but inaccurate – metaphor. Even after the exploding cannon, King Jim still had one leg more than a salmon.

Tudor terrors

> *Thou base football-player.*
> William Shakespeare, in *King Lear*

A puritan preacher in Tudor times said that football led to ungodliness … as if God never played football in her life, or Jesus had never made a good cross. He (the preacher, not Jesus) argued that …

> *Football-playing and other devilish pastimes withdraweth us from godliness, either upon the Sabbath or any other day.*
> Philip Stubbs, in *Anatomy of Abuses* (1583)

Stubbs was also concerned about the injuries that were taking their toll …

> *Sometimes their necks are broken, sometimes their backs, sometimes their legs, sometimes their arms, sometimes one part is thrust out of joint, sometimes the noses gush out with blood.*

Not a patch on the damage Stubbs's Puritan mates inflicted on the Catholics in the Tower of London torture chambers. The Tower tortures were carried out to eliminate the opposition and bring peace, whereas …

Football encourages envy and hatred, sometimes fighting, murder and a great loss of blood.

So not a lot changes then.

By Tudor times, football had evolved into a game you wouldn't want to play if you are of a delicate disposition. By the days of Henry VII and his Tudor brood, football was usually played between two villages. The aim was to capture the ball and take it back to your own village, any way you could. There were no other rules. As Stubbs explained:

Every player lies in wait to knock down the other players or punch them on the nose. There are no rules that I can tell. The man with the ball must run with it for his life.

Sometimes football was banned because fights broke out among the people *watching* the game. Is that what they mean by a 'spectator sport' I wonder?

Meanwhile, Henry VIII was like a few modern managers who can't find a settled team. They like to chop and change.

When fat Hen wanted a distraction, he didn't play peasant football, he played real tennis.[3] Playing tennis is what he chose to do when he wanted to take his mind off the harsh realities of life and death. Like the small matter of Wife No. 2, Anne Boleyn, having her head removed by a French swordsman. Henry went off to play tennis while his wife died. 'Love all', Henry cried (maybe) as the swordsman sliced his shot.

The year before Anne lost her head, a preacher said:

Football causes beastly fury and extreme violence.
Thomas Eliot, Puritan preacher (commenting in 1531)

So did being married to Henry the Ate. As Henry didn't say of Anne Boleyn …

He kept his head and buried it in the back of the net.
David Coleman (1926–2013), English sports commentator

But the Tudor Puritans were just warming up on the pitch. In 1540, people in England were banned from playing football – again.

---

3. Known, among other games, as the Sport of Kings. So, no revolting peasants raqueting around in the exclusive courts.

And two years later, another game was named and shamed and banned, the game called shuffleboard (shove-halfpenny). And can you wonder? A misplaced halfpenny could have someone's eye out.

By 1581, in the reign of Elizabeth I,[4] some enlightenment came in the unlikely guise of a schoolteacher who said that football is *good* for you.

> *Football is of great helps, both to health and strength. It strengtheneth and brawneth the whole body, and by provoking superfluities downward, it dischargeth the head, and upper parts, it is good for the bowels, and to drive the stone and gravel from both the bladder and kidneys.*[5]
>
> Richard Mulcaster, headmaster of Merchant Taylors' School
> (commenting in 1581)

Philip Stubbs may have had a point about the sport 'withdraweth us from godliness' because in 1589, Hugh Case and William Shurlock not only ignored the ban but played in the ungodliest place imaginable. They were fined 2 shillings for playing football in St Werburgh's cemetery during the vicar's sermon. Perhaps youthful thoughtlessness was their defence? After all …

> *I was a young lad when I was growing up.*
>
> David O'Leary (b. 1958), Irish football manager

But fines and arrests did not deter the determined. In 1576 in Ruislip, a report said that …

> *Around a hundred people assembled themselves unlawfully and played a certain unlawful game, called football.*

Uncivil war

> *Manchester, one of the greatest, if not really THE greatest mere village in England.*
>
> Daniel Defoe, in *A Tour Through the Whole Island of Great Britain*

---

4. Who did NOT rule from Crystal Palace, was never served in her forests by Queens Park Rangers but may have been known by the Scots as Queen of the South.
5. Loosely translated, it helps you spit, poo and pee.

That village of Manchester was a football hotspot from the start. In Manchester in 1608 …

A company of lewd and disordered persons broke many men's windows during an unlawful game of football.

It was such a major problem that within ten years, the Manchester Village Council appointed special 'football officers' to enforce the laws.

The village, since the Industrial Revolution, has grown large enough to have two big teams. As they are both from the same village, they are probably the best of friends, don't you think?

They are *professional* footballers, of course. And professionals play by the rules.

It's just a job. Grass grows, birds fly, waves pound the sand. I beat people up.

Muhammad Ali (1942–2016), American boxer

Meanwhile in Ireland …

Out of Ireland have we come, great hatred, little room, maimed us at the start. I carry from my mother's womb a fanatic heart.

William Butler Yeats

Kicking a stuffed pig's bladder around was a dangerous enough occupation. But after Ireland had been ravaged by Oliver Cromwell, the football turned far more gruesome.

Charles II came to the throne and restored some harmony. But cheerful Charlie's son, James II, was a secret Catholic who became king of England and Ireland.

James II gave Richard Talbot ('Lying Dick' Talbot) the job of turning the Protestant Irish army into a Catholic one.

Dim Jim II was thrown off his throne in England but fled to Ireland for help. The new (Protestant) king of England, William of Orange, set about taking Ireland back from Dim Jim and Lying Dick.

William's ally, Lord Galmoy, was annoyed when William's army drove him from Crom Castle. All he had were two young English prisoners to show for his troubles. He made sure they paid for his humiliation:

1. Captain Dixey and Cornet Charleton were hanged from an inn sign.
2. Their bodies were put on the kitchen table of the inn and their heads cut off.
3. The heads were kicked around the village like footballs.
4. The heads were finally nailed to the inn door.

If it was all done under the inn sign, we can imagine alcohol was partly to blame for the depravity. Alcohol and football have often gone hand in boot …

In 1969, I gave up women and alcohol – it was the worst twenty minutes of my life.

George Best (1946–2005), Irish footballer
(who played for a Manchester village team as well)

German Georgians

You'd have thought the German Georgian kings may have brought a more enlightened approach to football. But not much changed.

Football games were often organised in the street. Two sides booted a leather ball filled with air and weren't too bothered about how many windows they broke in houses and coaches. In Gloucester in 1811, the *Shrewsbury Chronicle* reported …

An apprentice was convicted of playing football on a Sunday. He was sentenced to 14 days in prison.

Just *one* apprentice? Was he too slow to run away from the local law officers?[6]

Victorian public schools

If the peasant games were rough, the players needed to know they were *lucky*. Because the upper classes had a tougher approach to their football games. A hack to an opponent's shins was an accepted tactic.

In the public schools, if the teachers didn't thrash you then the older boys (prefects) did. In the coaching world of the carrot and the stick, there were

---

6. Another writer might say, 'He paid the penalty'. Not me.

no actual carrots but very real sticks. A pupil from Harrow public school explained:

> *The bullying was terrible in our time. If the little boys could not keep up at football, then they were made to cut large thorn sticks from the hedges and flogged with them till the blood ran down their jerseys. I can truly say that I never learned anything useful at Harrow and had little chance of learning anything. Hours and hours were wasted on useless Latin verses. A boy's school education at this time was hopelessly stupid.*

I think we'd all prefer a hack to the shins any time.

Tackling the Truce – 1914

> *We didn't underestimate them – they were just a lot better than we thought.*
>
> Bobby Robson (1933–2009), England football manager

Sport has been known to encourage civility rather than hostility. Not very often, of course, but a famous example was at Christmas 1914 in the trenches of France and Flanders.

In 1914, a truce led to a football international that was a rare outbreak of peace between the Allies and the Axis powers – mainly Britain versus Germany.

> *Football is a simple game. Twenty-two men chase a ball for ninety minutes and at the end, the Germans always win.*
>
> Gary Lineker (b. 1960), England footballer, quoted after England were knocked out by Germany in the semi-finals of Italia '90.

At first, the British troops – the peasant cannon fodder of their generation – thought that candlelit German Christmas trees, raised on the parapets of their trenches, were a trick and shot them down. The Germans put them back up and the British stopped firing.

There were many reports of football matches between the enemies. Some were organised, and others were just friendly kickabouts with a hundred men joining in.

Some truces went on until New Year's Day but most ended after Boxing Day. In one part of the trenches the British politely told the Germans, 'We will start shooting again at nine o'clock.' The Germans called back, 'Then we'll come over to your trenches – we'll be safer.'

Many of the men found it hard to start fighting again. When their officers gave the order to shoot the enemy, the British soldiers replied, 'We can't – they are good fellows and we can't.'

The officers replied, 'If you don't start firing then we will – and it won't be at the Germans.'

The German troops had the same problem. For several days, the British and Germans fired at one another without trying to hit. A soldier wrote:

> *We spent that day and the next wasting ammunition in trying to shoot the stars from the sky.*

The generals on both sides were furious when they heard about the informal Christmas truces. As the First World War grew more bitter, a Christmas truce like 1914 would never be seen again.

And the results? Did the 'Germans always win'? It depends who you ask. Usually a one-all draw is the diplomatic conclusion.[7]

The Welsh wizards

Jonah was swallowed by a whale and came out singing. Well, all the best singers come from Wales, don't they? Some of the best football songs too …

1. *'Are you Llanfairpwllgwyngyllgogerychwyrndrobwllllantysiliogogogoch in disguise?'*
   (Wrexham FC)

2. *'Look out here comes a crowd of jolly fellows all looking gay*
   Bent on a visit to the football field to watch two teams play.'
   (Swansea FC, 1913)

3. *I can't read and I can't write*
   But that doesn't really matter,
   Coz I am from Carmarthen Town
   And I can drive a tractor.
   (Aberystwyth FC)

---

7. Fortunately, the result did not then go to penalties. It would be another hundred years before England won a penalty shoot-out in an international game.

4. (Tune: *Oh when the saints go marching in*)
   Oh fluffy sheep are wonderful
   Oh fluffy sheep are wonderful,
   They are white, Welsh and fluffy
   Oh fluffy sheep are wonderful.
   (Wales national team)

The French approach

> *He's got a knock on his shin there, just above the knee.*
> Frank Stapleton (b. 1956), Irish football player and manager

The English Football Association was formed in 1863 to formalise the rules and differentiate it from 'Rugby', which belonged to the public schools. The railways had brought mobility to the working classes and they could travel the country to support their teams. Leagues were formed, players became professional, rivalries grew and the working-class game became 'war minus the shooting'.

At first the game of football allowed a little handling but the biggest block to an agreed set of rules was the issue of 'hacking' the opponent's shins.

In 1863, Ebenezer Cobb Morley's code of rules allowed the 'hack to the front of the leg' of an opponent but he tried to outlaw the practice.

He argued that it was so childish …

if we have hacking, no mature player will play at football, and it will be entirely left to schoolboys.

Many supporters of the more boisterous entertainment believed charging, hacking, holding and tripping were important parts of the game. One supporter of hacking said that without it …

You will do away with the courage and pluck of the game, and it will be bound to bring over a lot of Frenchmen who would beat you with a week's practice.

Football Association meeting, representative from Blackheath

(A lot of Frenchmen beating a British team? That'll never happen. Remember Waterloo.)

Ebenezer Cobb Morley got his way … probably a sharp kick in the shins (or the crotch) of the Blackheath rep resolved the argument.

Meanwhile, the rugger chaps abandoned the old football maxim …

Kick the ball if you can and if you can't, kick the other man's shins.

The forked paths of football and rugby went their separate ways.

In 1872, the first FA cup was played, and the final held … you've guessed it … at The Oval cricket ground. By the time Queen Vic died, and the twentieth century dawned, the top levels of the game were dominated by professionals.

The peasants were reduced to the role of spectators … and hooligans. They are still at it.

A Newcastle United football fan who punched a police horse in the head during a riot in April 2013 said in his defence:

I love animals – I've got three dogs, a fish pond out the back and I feed foxes across the road.

He added:

I would like to apologize to the horse.[8]

Nice to know he doesn't (apparently) punch his fish – thank cod. Fish suffer enough from being battered. A judge with horse sense jailed him for twelve months.

Classy cricket

I tend to think that cricket is the greatest thing that God ever created on earth – certainly greater than sex, although sex isn't too bad either.
Harold Pinter (1930–2008), British playwright

Stoolball was a sport dating back to at least the 1400s. It seems to have originated in Sussex, southern England, and evolved (probably) into cricket.

The cricketing folklore says it was played by milkmaids who used their milking stools as a three-legged 'wicket' and their milk bowls as bats. 'Playing stoolball' became a euphemism for sex – Shakespeare and Fletcher use the term 'playing stool ball' to mean just that in *Two Noble Kinsmen*.

---

8. You couldn't make it up, and, I assure you, I am NOT.

Cricket developed from a children's game when noblemen used adult teams to make wagers.[9] It was not quite in the same league as prize fighting and horse racing when it came to gambling – their lordships liked to join in the games of cricket. But gambling was the engine in the machine. The first newspaper report of a match was in 1697 and it was the betting that mattered more than the score …

The middle of last week a great match at cricket was played in Sussex; there were eleven of a side, and they played for fifty guineas apiece.

Foreign Post

The noble amateurs employed professional 'Players' they called 'local experts' to play alongside them as teammates. Edward 'Lumpy' Stevens was employed as a gardener by His Lordship in the off season and as an ace bowler on the cricket pitch. 'Lumpy' probably got his name because bowlers were allowed to select the pitch they played on and Stevens opted for the one that was bumpy; if he pitched the ball on the downward slope of a 'lump' it would be hard for a batsman to defend. One of cricket's earliest odes was dedicated to Stevens's use of this technique:

For honest Lumpy did allow
He ne'er would pitch but o'er a brow.

Arthur Haygarth (1825–1903),
in *Scores and Biographies*

A story has been repeated by former British Prime Minister John Major that 'Lumpy' joined the army and followed his heroism on the cricket field with heroism on the battlefield, when he deflected a cannonball away from the head of an officer. (How's that? I hear you cry.)

Gentlemen and players may have shared the field as teammates, but *never* as equals. One early twentieth-century historian suggested that the intermingling of the powerful with their peasants led to social stability … all boys together.

If the French noblesse had been capable of playing cricket with their peasants, their chateaux would never have been burnt.

G.M. Trevelyan (1876–1962), British historian

---

9. And where there's gambling there's match-fixing. As early as 1806, a professional, William Lambert, received a lifetime ban for rigging a game. In the 2020s, there are still many players serving life bans.

And so the lines were drawn between Gentlemen and Players. The working-class amateurs (the Players) were clearly not Gentlemen and were expected to know their place. Cricket made no attempt to disguise the apartheid between the classes.

⇨ Professional 'Players' were often treated much as servants would be, and were expected to be as deferential to amateurs as a butler would be to the master of the house.

⇨ The 'Gentlemen' amateurs insisted upon separate dressing rooms.

⇨ At some grounds they even had a separate gateway onto the field.

⇨ On scorecards, the amateur would be listed initials first and a professional teammate initials last: for example, O.S.O. Posh and Slob, A.

⇨ Any team with an amateur in the side would appoint him as captain, even though he may be the weakest player.[10]

⇨ Professional player/coaches were employed by public schools to teach boys many years their junior, but were expected to call the boys 'sir'.

The astonishing thing is that the demarcation went on until 1962. Even then, the abolition of the Gentleman status in the game – like the abolition of the slave trade – was met with howls and lamentations from the dinosaurs. One lordly participant said that the 'Gentlemen' ethos had value and would in time be seen as a loss to society. Peasants of fifty years later may disagree.

In 1997, a Labour politician tried to persuade us all that social apartheid, like Gentlemen and Players, was dead.

> *We are all middle class now.*
> John Prescott, Labour politician (b. 1938)

The national cricket psyche

> *I do love cricket – it's so very English.*
> Sarah Bernhardt (1844–1923), French stage actress

Sir Henry Newbolt (1862–1938) was a lawyer and a poet who championed the virtues of chivalry and sportsmanship combined in the service of the British Empire.

---

10. A hangover from the concept of the Officer Class in the army – let the other-rank peasants do the fighting while the gentlemen send them to their deaths.

In 1897, he wrote a poem about a schoolboy cricketer who grows up to fight in Africa, *Vitai Lampada*. Cricket is portrayed as a noble fight to the end:

> *THERE'S a breathless hush in the Close to-night –*
> *Ten to make and the match to win –*
> *A bumping pitch and a blinding light,*
> *An hour to play and the last man in.*
> *And it's not for the sake of a ribboned coat,*
> *Or the selfish hope of a season's fame,*
> *But his Captain's hand on his shoulder smote*
> *'Play up! play up! and play the game!'*

Years later, confronted with a real fight to the death he summons up the memory of that cricket match to battle on against the odds:

> *The sand of the desert is sodden red, –*
> *Red with the wreck of a square that broke; –*
> *The Gatling's jammed and the colonel dead,*
> *And the regiment blind with dust and smoke.*
> *The river of death has brimmed his banks,*
> *And England's far, and Honour a name,*
> *But the voice of schoolboy rallies the ranks,*
> *'Play up. play up. and play the game.'*

Henry Newbolt (1862–1938), English writer

The poem was publicly acclaimed at the time of its publication, in the days of the Boer War, 1898.

It was revived at the outbreak of the First World War, when optimism was high. *Vitai Lampada* inspired the Gentlemen officers as well as the Player Tommies to fight on. Like Newbolt's cricketer, the worse the odds, the more noble the fight.

It took the terror of the trenches to disillusion both Gentlemen and Players. It took yet another war to abolish the Gentlemen v. Players fixtures and customs.

Newbolt came to dislike his most famous poem. He was constantly called upon to recite the poem and by 1923, sighed …

It's a kind of Frankenstein's Monster that I created thirty years ago.

Sarah Bernhardt may have been right. The British are steeped in the ethos of cricket. A man or a woman stands alone, armed only with a bat to defend his castle while besieged by hostile forces.

And, with the image of the brave Brits standing alone, comes the vestigial (but enduring) feeling that a peasant may be a great player, but a gentleman will always be captain of the team.

The national teams

Britain has three national sports – soccer, rugby and cricket – and each sport became a microcosm of society. Spooky thought. And even scarier, maybe it always will.

A Victorian summed it up well … he was an outsider – a Jew – so maybe he had a better perspective than his fellow politicians when he described Britain as …

> *Two nations between whom there is no intercourse and no sympathy; who are as ignorant of each other's habits, thoughts, and feelings, as if they were dwellers in different zones, or inhabitants of different planets. The rich and the poor.*

Benjamin Disraeli (1804–1881),
British politician and writer, in his novel *Sybil*

Chapter 9

Warfare

Man's inhumanity to man makes countless thousands mourn.
Robert Burns (1759–1796), Scottish poet and lyricist

Man's inhumanity to Frenchmen

The Hundred Years War (which lasted 116 years) was the height of chivalry and inhumaneness. Battles like Agincourt and Poitiers were mythologised as the gallant little English and Welsh forces against the massed ranks of the cream of the French military machine.

Certainly, William Shakespeare would like you to think that. But he wrote plays like *Henry V* for a Tudor monarch (Welsh ancestry) and bigged up the part of the Welsh archers. That's just one of the many legends that Shakespeare helped create.

There are a few myths about the Battle of Agincourt (1415) that you may like to dispel over a pint of lemonade in the pub. 'Once more unto the breach, dear friends …'

⇨ The huge French numerical advantage? The chronicler from Burgundy, Jean de Wavrin, gives the total French army size as 50,000. Not realistic for mediaeval times. Modern estimates say around 12,000 French to 8,000 English and Welsh.

⇨ The 'V' sign originated at Agincourt? It has been attributed to the battle of Agincourt: legend has it that the French threatened to cut off the fingers of any captured English archers to stop them firing their bows. The peasant archers held up those two fingers in a defiant 'V' sign. A moment's thought will tell us that it would be just as effective to cut the grubby throats of the archers. There are no records of dislodged digits from the time of the battle.

⇨ It was the Welsh archers what won it? Around 460 Welsh soldiers left Wales; their numbers were thinned yet further by disease at Harfleur. It is likely that only about 400 actually fought at the battle in an army of around 8,000. A ten-year rebellion had ravaged Wales and the English distrusted them for many years after. The Welsh at that time were forbidden to hold land or public offices in England. It's surprising that any soldiers were enlisted from Wales at all.

⇨ The massacre of defeated French prisoners at the end? A slaughter of the French prisoners was said to follow the battle. Henry V was worried the huge number of prisoners would realise they outnumbered the guarding troops and resume fighting. Only the highest ranks were spared because they were worth more in ransom. Legend or lies? Looking at the ransom contracts it seems they were for all ranks, not just the super-rich. If that's a lie, then so too would be the scale of the slaughter. Some prisoners were killed, not hundreds.

Myths, but we do like our myths, so they persist.

Legend remains victorious in spite of history.

Sarah Bernhardt

One tale that is quite believable is that the English knights found it contrary to chivalry to kill prisoners. So, who got the job of slitting throats? The archers and foot soldiers – it was the peasants who had blood on their hands. And, outside the heat of battle, jabbing a jugular must have made even the most hardened peasant a little squeamish.

It's said the foot soldiers found knights floundering in the mud of the battlefield unable to rise in their armour. They used a thin, razor-sharp knife to slide between the joints in the armour and despatch the armoured enemies. Even the French would say *'C'est la guerre'*. But to take a knife to an unarmed man, weary and defeated after the battle, must have been different, don't you think?

The peasant foot soldier couldn't refuse. Henry V threatened to hang anyone who did not obey his mandate to murder. An interesting dilemma. If a monarch ordered YOU to kill an enemy in cold blood, or be hanged, what would you do?

Reluctant peasants

Man is the unnatural animal, the rebel child of nature, and more and more does he turn himself against the harsh and fitful hand that reared him.

H.G. Wells (1866–1946), English author

141

Just over a hundred years before Agincourt, the Welsh peasant foot soldiers had been a bolshie bunch. Wales was a poor country in the 1200s and after a failed rebellion in the late 1200s, they were under the heel of the Norman-English and their feudal rule. But they were on the road to rebellion.

⇨ 1267: Henry III of England made Llywelyn ap Gruffydd the 'Prince of Wales'. This is a cynical piece of patronising because Henry only wants to stop Llywelyn attacking England. Llewelyn naturally thinks of himself as 'Prince of Wales'. That's fine so long as he doesn't get above himself.

⇨ 1274: Edward I became king of England and set about making Wales part of England. He ignored Henry III's peace, he hated Llywelyn and battered the Welsh. He even had Llywelyn's bride, Eleanor, kidnapped on the way to the wedding.[1]

⇨ 1282: Llywelyn, now Prince of Wales, had to fight to keep Wales for the Welsh. In 1282, he rebelled against King Edward of England. He burned Edward's castles and fought Edward's troops. Edward was furious. But while Llywelyn was away gathering a new army, the English attacked first. The Welsh were beaten near Builth Wells. They say 3,000 Welsh surrendered and put down their weapons – then the English slaughtered them. Llywelyn heard the battle and rushed back. But it was a trap. He'd been betrayed.[2] Llywelyn wasn't wearing any armour – just a tunic. An English knight, Stephen de Frankton, charged at him with a lance, then cut off Llywelyn's head. It was put on show in English towns.

⇨ England ruled Wales. The Welsh – like lanced Llewelyn – had no head. English Ed built massive castles to make sure it stayed that way.

⇨ 1287: The Welsh peasants, however, resented that Norman-English rule and rebelled. They failed.[3] But the Welsh resentment didn't go away.

⇨ 1294: The English demanded an unpopular tax – does that sound a familiar provocation to a peasants' revolt? The tax was to pay for

---

1. Don't worry ... Llywelyn and Eleanor got together in the end and lived happy ever after and all that. Sort of. She died giving birth to their only baby, and Eleanor wasn't too happy ever after that.
2. Who betrayed him? Some say the Bishop of Bangor and some say a blacksmith of Builth. But a top suspect is Dafydd, Llewelyn's own brother. If so, you may be pleased to know that Dafydd was treated as a traitor by the English then hanged, drawn and quartered at Shrewsbury market cross.
3. Wat Tyler's 'Peasants' Revolt' of 1381 is one of those history signposts on the road through time ... along with 1066, Magna Carta, Bosworth Field and so on. Yet this Welsh rebellion is forgotten. Could it be because British education is really English education and the Welsh don't matter ... and Welsh peasant events matter least of all? Just asking.

Edward's wars in France. But the Welsh were forced to pay a tax far higher than their English neighbours.

⇨ The English coupled that tax with the conscription of Welsh troops for Edward's campaign in Gascony. The Welsh archers had the skill but loathed the obligation. Of course, you can see Edward's b-i-g mistake, can't you? The Welsh peasants not only hated the English … now they were armed. Armed by the English. Oh, Edward, couldn't you predict what would happen next? What sort of idiot aggravates a mob and then weaponises them?

⇨ 30 September 1294 and (seething) Welsh soldiers were assembled at Shrewsbury. They were due to march to Portsmouth for Edward's campaign in Gascony. They mutinied and killed their English officers. The rebels rallied around a distant cousin of Llywelyn, Madog ap Llywelyn, and several Welsh castles were put under siege.

⇨ Edward abandoned his plans to invade France and turned north-west to deal with the rebels. He offered the Welsh foot soldiers a deal: 'Fight for England in France and you will be pardoned.' Madog offered them a different sort of deal: 'Fight for the English hundreds of miles from home or fight for your homeland.' Which did the Welsh choose? They chose to fight against the English.

⇨ The peasant rebels faced the might of English armour and warhorses. A porcupine hedge of spears, planted in the ground, worked well at first but eventually they were overcome by power … and sneakiness. A picked party of English archers, led by a few knights, made a sortie against the rebel camp at midnight. The Welsh, who were literally caught napping, lost 500 men. After six months of struggle, they were smashed by the might of Edward's army and Madog was captured.[4]

It's an interesting insight into the peasant philosophy: the peasants chose defence of Wales over fighting in foreign fields; the peasants' heartstrings were tied to their birthplace.

> *I think the answer lies in the soil.*
> Kenneth Williams's character Farmer Arthur
> Fallowfield, in the radio comedy *Beyond Our Ken*

---

4. Madog should have been disembowelled as a traitor just as Dafydd had been before him. But, for some reason, Edward spared his life – and his guts – and simply kept him prisoner in the Tower of London. His Scottish opposite number – William Wallace – was not so fortunate and died a traitor's death.

Rotten rebels

There were many riots and rebellions after the 1381 Peasants' Revolt, of course. They arose among the peasants of the countryside but found less and less support from the underclasses in the towns. Without rural and urban rebels uniting they had little chance of success ... though they left a blood-soaked trail.

1450 Jack Cade's Rebellion in Kent

The Men of Kent started it off again. They'd started the 1381 Peasants' Revolt. This time they were led by Jack Cade. Like Wat Tyler before him, Cade's origins are obscure ...

> *When beggars die, there are no comets seen; the heavens themselves blaze forth the death of princes.*
>
> William Shakespeare, in *Julius Caesar*

And when a peasant is born there is no comet seen and no chronicles to record the fact. As Cade used a variety of aliases, there is no certainty that his birth date, place or name could be tracked down anyway.

If the facts are thin on the ground, then the legends and rumours fill in the gaps.

⇨ Historians are fairly sure Cade was low-born ... but according to others, he was Dr Alymere, son-in-law of a Surrey squire, and still others believed he was a practitioner of witchcraft. Or he wasn't.
⇨ Jack Cade became a fugitive from justice after he murdered a pregnant woman. Or he didn't.
⇨ He was an agent of Richard of York generating dissent to back the Yorkist claim to the throne ... or he wasn't.
⇨ Jack Cade was born in Sussex ... or he wasn't.
⇨ Jack Cade was born between 1420 and 1430 ... probably.

Almost certainly, the peasants of England were dissatisfied with the gentry losing the wars with France and raising the threat of invasion. The English defending army in the south were poorly resourced so they took to helping themselves to the stores from the towns. Looting their own people.

When the corpse of the king's close ally, the Duke of Suffolk, was washed up on the shore at Dover, the king blamed the people of the county. The people of Kent faced reprisals. Cade persuaded the peasants to get their retaliation in first and 5,000 marched on London to demand an end to the corruption in the government.

They also wanted to right the wrongs of the old peasant grievance – the Statute of Labourers, which made peasants subject to compulsory labour. It was a tax designed purely to benefit the landowning class.

Fighting to tax the community for the advantage of a class is not protection: it is plunder.

Benjamin Disraeli

Cade and his followers defeated a royal army at Sevenoaks in Kent and entered London, where they executed Sir James Fiennes, the Lord Treasurer. That's what you call a tax cut. They also decapitated Sir James's son-in-law, William Crowmer. The heads of Fiennes and Crowmer were placed on stakes and paraded through town, face to face in a parody of kissing each other.

Despite Cade's attempt to keep his men under control, once the rebel forces had entered London they began to loot. And Cade joined in. Maybe not the brightest thing to do.

Those who fight corruption should be clean themselves.

Vladimir Putin (b. 1952), Russian statesman

Naturally the looting alienated the people of London. The very people who had been sympathetic to the revolt now turned against the rebel rabble. The king, Henry VI, didn't have to raise an army – his London citizens did the fighting for him.

The rebels were forced out of the city in a bloody battle on London Bridge. To end the bloodshed the rebels were issued pardons by the king and told to return home. Henry VI revoked Cade's personal pardon though. Oh dear …

Put not your trust in princes, nor in the son of man, in whom there is no help.[5]

King James Bible, Psalm 146:3

---

5. A contemporary translation is more chatty, but less sonorous: 'You can't depend on anyone, not even a great leader.' And Henry VI was a l-o-n-g way from being a great leader.

Cade fled but was later cornered in a garden by Alexander Iden, a future High Sheriff of Kent.

In the skirmish that followed, Cade was mortally wounded and died before reaching London for trial. But that didn't stop the lords having his body hanged, having his guts cut out and burned, being beheaded then cut into quarters.

Cade's head was displayed in London. Unlike his treasury victims, Cade had no one to kiss.

The other leaders suffered the same fate and the bits of their bodies were sent around England as a warning to others.

Shakespeare may have said that the lives of princes are celebrated in the heavens. Yet humble Jack Cade is immortalised as a character in the play *Henry VI Part 2* ... by William Shakespeare.

> JACK CADE *Be brave, then; for your captain is brave, and vows reformation. There shall be in England seven half-penny loaves sold for a penny: the three-hoop'd pot shall have ten hoops; and I will make it felony to drink small beer: all the realm shall be in common; and in Cheapside shall my palfrey go to grass: and when I am king,– as king I will be,–*
>
> ALL *God save your majesty.*
>
> JACK CADE *I thank you, good people:– there shall be no money; all shall eat and drink on my score; and I will apparel them all in one livery, that they may agree like brothers, and worship me their lord.*
>
> DICK *The first thing we do, let's kill all the lawyers.*
>
> William Shakespeare, *Henry VI Part 2*

That last line has found a lot of sympathy around the world for 400 years.

Shakespeare's Cade seems to have delusions of becoming king ... and of it being a bit of a walkover ...

> JACK CADE: *For our enemies shall fall before us, inspired with the spirit of putting down kings and princes*
>
> William Shakespeare, *Henry VI Part 2*

The Cade Rebellion was better remembered than the Welsh Madog revolt. Three hundred years after Cade was left kissing fresh air, the ghost of Cade still haunted the British establishment.

James Otis Jr. (1725–1783) was an American lawyer who generated the rebel catchphrase 'Taxation without representation is tyranny'. His British enemies urged King George III to charge Otis with treason – a crime only cured by execution.

The British prime minister called James Otis the 'Jack Cade of the Rebellion'. The shadow of Cade was a long one.

1549 Kett's Rebellion in Norfolk

If an injustice requires you to be the agent of injustice to another, then, I say, break the law. Let your life be a counter-friction to stop the government machine.

Henry David Thoreau (1817–1862), American author

Peasants had always survived by having 'common' land that everyone in their village shared. They could keep a cow there for milk or a few sheep for the wool.

In Tudor times, the rich and greedy landowners started grabbing the common land, 'enclosing' it behind fences and keeping the peasants off. This injustice was to cause trouble for hundreds of years to come.

In Wymondham, Norfolk, Robert Kett led a riot, tearing down the hedges and fences that made the enclosures. It turned into a full-scale rebellion as he gathered an army and attacked Norwich.

We know rather more about Kett than Cade. He was born in the Norfolk town of Wymondham to a middle-class family and made a large amount of money in business.

In 1549, the local commoners rose in revolt against what they saw as the injustices of Edward VI's government. Their first act was to tear down the symbols of those enclosures – the fences.

When the rebels arrived to pull down his fences, Kett listened to their arguments. Everyone loves a good Damascene conversion. The original was Saul in the Bible.

And suddenly a light from heaven flashed around him and he fell to the ground and heard a voice saying to him, 'Saul, Saul, why are you persecuting and oppressing Me?' And Saul said, 'Who are You, Lord?' And He answered, 'I am Jesus whom you are persecuting. Now get up and go into the city, and you will be told what you must do.'

King James Bible, Acts 9

Robert Kett 'saw the light' and helped the riotous mob to pull down his own fences. From that point, Robert Kett became the leader of the rebellion. The rebels marched towards Norwich, gathering support as they went. By the time they reached the gates of the city they were several thousand strong.

The burghers of the city refused to let them enter – and so Kett led his men to camp on Mousehold Heath and started to negotiate. Thousands more flocked to join his camp. The worried leaders of Norwich went out to meet Kett and ask for peace. They were met by a boy who dropped his trousers and showed them his backside. An enterprising and skilful archer sent an arrow into the boy's bum. It gives a whole new meaning to the phrase 'archery butt'.

King Edward VI's government intervened and told the city to close its gates to the rebels and prepare to defend itself.[6]

Kett's army had just one cannon yet managed to set fire to Norwich's 'Cow Tower' ... you could call it a bullseye.

Kett attacked the city and captured it, then set up a form of local court that would hear the cases brought to it by the commoners. The court was held in the open, underneath the 'tree of reformation'. Many money-grabbing, land-enclosing gents were dragged before it to be tried, found guilty and imprisoned. Kett's Rebellion spread from Norwich and soon the whole of East Anglia was in open revolt.

The government sent an army, led by the Marquis of Northampton, but the soldiers were no match for the rebels. The royal army was thrashed. As you'd expect, the government sent a much larger army to Norwich.

Nothing in this world can take the place of persistence. Persistence and determination alone are omnipotent.

Calvin Coolidge (1872–1933), American President

This new army was commanded by the Earl of Warwick. It entered the city and forced the rebels back onto Mousehold Heath. But he now found himself inside the city and besieged by over 15,000 outside.

Each night the rebels would come down from the heath, break into the city, gather supplies and attack Warwick's soldiers. Finally, government reinforcements arrived. Kett decided to gamble everything on one big battle at a small valley called Dussindale. The rebels had numbers but, as

---

6. Edward was only 11 years old and it was Edward Seymour, the Duke of Somerset, who mainly got the blame for these changes.

with the Welsh rebellions, not the cavalry. The rebels fled in the face of the charging horses and thousands were slaughtered. Thousands more were taken prisoner.

If a man smite you on one cheek, smash him down; smite him hip and thigh, for self-preservation is the highest law.

Might Is Right, or The Survival of the Fittest,
book by pseudonymous author Ragnar Redbeard (1890)

When Kett was finally defeated, forty-nine of his men were hanged in a day. They had to climb a ladder with a rope around their neck. The ladder would be taken away and they'd be left to swing. In Norwich that day, so many were hanged, the ladder was wrecked.

Robert Kett was captured a few miles away and taken to London. He was held in the Tower, tried and found guilty of treason. He was sentenced to be executed. He was then taken back to Norwich for his execution.

He was hung in chains from the walls of Norwich Castle and left to die of hunger and cold. The order said:

His body shall hang there until he should fall down on his own.

His body was left hanging there for many months as a reminder to the people of Norwich of the fate that awaited traitors. The victorious Seymour gloated …

Kett, with three other chief captains, all vile persons, are still held to receive that which they have deserved. We trust, truly, that these rebellions are now at an end.

Edward Seymour, Duke of Somerset (1500–1552), in a letter

He did not gloat for long. Two years later, Somerset was blamed by his noble peers for the social unrest in the country and beheaded on Tower Hill. King Edward VI did not raise a finger to help his 'Protector'.

Kett is revered as a hero of the people; Seymour is despised as a self-seeking chancer. Just because you lose it doesn't make you a loser.

Then let us all do what is right, strive with all our might toward the unattainable, develop as fully as we can the gifts God has given us, and never stop learning.

Ludwig van Beethoven (1770–1827), German composer

1607 The Captain Pouch Rising in the Midlands

Age is not important unless you're a cheese.

Helen Hayes (1900–1993), American actress

Sixty years passed and Kett's body had rotted to dust. Edward VI, Mary Tudor and Elizabeth I – the last of the Tudors – reigned and then went to that great palace in the sky where, presumably, they were outranked.

The Armada came, they saw and they sank, Guy Fawkes's Powder Plot sizzled then fizzled. Yet still the enclosures drove the underclasses to rebel.

Trouble broke out next in the Midlands. The leader was John Reynolds, an uneducated tinker from Northamptonshire. But like Tyler and Kett before him, he had a charisma that persuaded peasants to follow him. John was nicknamed Captain Pouch and a report of the time explained …

He was given the name Pouch because of a great leather pouch which he wore by his side. In this pouch he swore to his followers he held the power to defend them against all their enemies.

The tinker encouraged the disgruntled peasants to tear down the enclosure fences. They'd be fine. He had the authority of King James AND from God.

Three thousand protesters joined him in Warwickshire and another 5,000 in Leicestershire. The authorities in Leicester imposed a curfew on the townsfolk as they were afraid the citizens would rush out of the city to join the riots. A gibbet was erected as a warning to the illiterate who couldn't read a proclamation 'Do you want to end up here?'

It was pulled down by the illiterate citizens.

The educated differ from the uneducated as much as the living from the dead.

Aristotle (384–322 BC), Greek philosopher[7]

Women and children were more evident in Pouch's protests than they had been in previous revolts. Pouch told his army not to use violence – the exception to the rule being fences, of course – and his peasant army were armed with sticks and stones. King James I ordered that the ragtag army be

---

7. Yes, Aristotle was a clever bloke, but you can't help thinking that he (the educated) was the ultimate snob, demeaning the uneducated.

destroyed. By then, Captain Pouch was already in custody, so the peasants were without their leader for the final battle.

Routing them was no great military feat. The rebels were reminiscent of the First World War soldiers who sang to the tune of *The Church's One Foundation*:

> *We are Fred Karno's army,*
> *Fred Karno's infantry;*
> *We cannot fight, we cannot shoot,*
> *So what damn good are we?*

The Tresham family in Northamptonshire were the most aggressive enclosers. Sir Thomas Tresham was known as:

> *The most odious man in the county.*

When he called out the local militia, they refused to fight for him. Instead, the local landowners had to enlist their servants and arm them. The royal proclamation was read to the fence wreckers. The rioters carried on, so the landowners ordered their ad hoc army to charge on horseback using their swords against sticks and stones.

Forty to fifty were killed in the defences of the fences. Pouch and three of his followers were then hanged and quartered. The government promised to make life better for the revolting peasants. Just two months after the uprising, King James ordered a royal inquiry into the state of enclosure, which led to several landlords being prosecuted, and fined. However, none of the land was returned to common grazing. Effectively, they broke their promises.

Shakespeare had been involved in a land deal where enclosure became an issue. He summed up the grievances of the peasantry eloquently (as you would expect):

> *The rich ne'er cared for us, yet suffer us to famish, and their store-houses, crammed with grain.*
>
> William Shakespeare, in *Coriolanus*

The Pouch Rebellion was one of the last times that the rural peasantry of England and the gentry were in open conflict.

A sad failure. And the saddest symbol was the famous pouch carrying the token from God and the king. When Reynolds was caught and the pouch was opened, what was found inside? A piece of mouldy cheese.

Chapter 10

Education

Education is what remains after one has forgotten what one has learned in school.

Albert Einstein

Schooling

Mediaeval education in England was the preserve of the rich. Education in mediaeval England had to be paid for and mediaeval peasants could not have hoped to have afforded the fees.

Gradually the middle classes began to generate the wealth to create schools that would educate their children. By 1500, many large towns had a grammar school. These schools were very small, perhaps just one room for all the boys. Girls? Why would a girl need to read or write? Spinning and weaving, sewing and cooking? They can be taught by her mother.

The usual staffing was one teacher … who invariably had a religious background. This teacher would teach the older boys who were then responsible for teaching the younger ones.

That was a system that would influence the schooling of peasants, when it eventually became universal.

Lessons could start at sunrise and finish at sunset. Discipline was very strict.

All punishment is mischief; all punishment in itself is evil.

Jeremy Bentham (1748–1832), English
philosopher and social reformer

Mistakes in lessons were punished with the birch and it was open house to allow sadists to enjoy their hobby …

I know one master who, in winter, would on a cold morning whip his boys for no other reason than to warm himself up. Another beat them for swearing, and all the while he swore himself with horrible oaths.

Henry Peachum (1578–1644), English poet and schoolmaster at
Kimbolton Grammar School

Masters could swear, pupils couldn't. Punishments for the offence could be incorporated into the school rules.

> *It is ordered that for every oath or rude word spoken, in the school or elsewhere, the scholar shall have three strokes of the cane.*
>
> Manchester Grammar School rules (1528)

The brutality of birching led to at least one case of schadenfreude. A teacher destroyed his own birch over the backside of some boys and needed new twigs. The most supple – and painful – were at the ends of the branches. On the tree he chose, those twigs hung over the river. When he climbed along the branch to cut the twigs, it snapped. He fell in the river and drowned.

For some reason the pupils made no attempt to save him.

The landowners and lords knew the simple fact that Literacy is power.[1]

> *Be careful about reading health books. You may die of a misprint.*
>
> Mark Twain

The sons of the peasants could only be educated if the lord of the manor had given his permission. If a peasant family was caught having a son educated without permission, they were heavily fined. An educated peasant might prove a threat to his master as he might start to ask questions about big ideas like 'democracy', 'human rights', 'liberty, equality and fraternity'.[2]

> *The said truth is that it is the greatest happiness of the greatest number that is the measure of right and wrong.*
>
> Jeremy Bentham

Illiterate peasants were the norm in the Middle Ages and long after. Some of the giants of the 1800s' Industrial Revolution were illiterate peasants … people like George Stephenson. He didn't need to be literate to design and build steam locomotives, survey the railway lines and change the world.

---

1. During the American Civil War, it became a crime to teach a slave to read. So, the mediaeval principle of keeping the underclasses illiterate was extant 500 years later.
2. The illiterate French peasants couldn't spell those words, but they knew what they meant. And they came up with a new word for overbearing nobility: 'Guillotine'.

Vicious Victorians

But it was the Industrial Revolution that led to universal schooling ... in an unplanned way.

⇨ The machines drove the rural cottage industries out of business and the peasants migrated to the towns to work in the factories.
⇨ The rural peasants had watched over their children as they laboured in the fields and homes, but the factories offered no childcare. The children went into the factories with their parents.
⇨ Those children were exploited as cheap labour until humanists vented their rage on the cruelties and the losses of childhood.
⇨ Children were gradually banned from the factories but there was still no childcare for the majority.
⇨ The children wandered the streets, caused trouble and the crime rates rose. (Judges were oddly reluctant to have a child hanged for petty crimes even though the law allowed it.)[3]

In 1857, a new law was passed, and it came up with a new way of punishing little criminals who did little crimes. What was this new punishment?

The little devils were sent to school.

That's right – as a PUNISHMENT, children were sent to SCHOOL. 'The Industrial Schools Act' of 1857 let judges send children from 7 to 14 to 'Industrial Schools' where they would be taught reading and writing and learn useful skills like sewing and woodwork. In 1861, the law said the 'Industrial Schools' should be used for ...

⇨ any child under 14 caught begging
⇨ any child found wandering homeless
⇨ any child found with a gang of thieves
⇨ any child under 12 who has committed a crime
⇨ any child under 14 whose parents say s/he is out of control.

The long sentences were designed to break the child away from the 'bad influences' of home and environment.

Since then, many millions have seen enforced schooling as a custodial sentence.

---

3. Reluctant, but it was an option. In 1801, a boy of 13 was hanged for breaking into a house and stealing a spoon. In 1808, two sisters were hanged in Lynn for theft. One was aged 11. Her little sister was just 8. Then, in 1831, just six years before Victoria took the throne, a 9-year-old boy was hanged at Chelmsford for setting fire to a house.

Did you know ...?

Children could be punished for doing nothing, other than 'loitering'. One boy's story is typical:

> *I was born in Wisbech near Cambridge. My mother died when I was five and my father married again. My stepmother hated me so I ran away.*
>
> *I lived by begging and sleeping rough and made my way to London. There I'd sleep on doorsteps or anywhere that gave a little shelter. I suffered terribly from hunger and at times I thought I'd starve. I got crusts but I can hardly tell how I lived.*
>
> *One night I was sleeping under a railway bridge when a policeman came along and asked me what I was up to. I told him I had no place to go and he said I had to go with him.*
>
> *Next morning, he took me to court and told the judge there were always a lot of boys living under the bridge. They were young thieves and they gave a lot of trouble. I was mixing with them, so I was given fourteen days in prison.*
>
> *I'll carry on begging and go from workhouse to workhouse to sleep. I am unhappy but I have to get used to it.*

By the 1860s, the government decided the best way to deal with the problem of feral children was to lock them up in a sort of prison all day. But of course, they couldn't *call* it that. They called the detention centres 'schools'.

The government copied the upper-class tradition of dealing with unemployable children and opened state schools. They claimed they were 'educating' the masses but that was a sham.

The big lie – perpetuated to this day – is that the government provides 'education'. In fact, it merely provides 'schooling'. It keeps children off the streets.

The Elementary Education Act of 1870 enforced schooling for all children from the ages of 5 to 12 in England and Wales. With more than 100 pupils in some classrooms, the idea of tailoring the teaching to the individual was unthinkable.

Paying the price

When more of the people's sustenance is exacted through the form of taxation than is necessary, such exaction becomes ruthless extortion and a violation of the fundamental principles of free government.

Grover Cleveland

The education provided under the 1870 Act was not free. A family had to pay a few pence a week for each child attending.

The children of poor families were no longer allowed to work to pay their way in the factories and mines, so the parents were forced to pay to keep their children off the streets. Pennies per week don't sound much to us, but for poorer families this became a terrible burden. As well as the payment there was the loss of their children's income while they attended school.

But there was no way round this. In an extension of the law, in 1880, school boards were required to enforce attendance … whether that family could afford the rate or not.

In 1883, a Leicester head teacher moaned:

I generally find some parents frequently keep their children away from school on the most trivial and frivolous excuses.

But very often the excuses were neither trivial nor frivolous. It was a matter of survival. Truancy among girls was especially high because they were kept away to help out in the home – care for younger siblings, perhaps, while the mother made some much-needed income to pay for the schooling of the older ones.

And truancy increased when seasonal work came along. At a Birmingham school the inspectors discovered several children flogging Christmas novelties on the streets. That would earn the extra coppers to improve the Christmas cheer of the family. The head teachers would rather the child was in school, learning some historical facts on a topic they would never need in their life. Mr Scrooge would have approved. Oh, what head teacher could begrudge a child its Christmas? A teacher who was …

Hard and sharp as flint, from which no steel had ever struck out generous fire; secret, and self-contained, and solitary as an oyster.

Charles Dickens, in *A Christmas Carol*

Many of the excuses were genuine hardship … children who couldn't attend school because they had no winter boots to walk through the icy streets.

Failure of the child to attend school would result in a visit from an inspector and a fine for the family. And attending school resulted in a good reference – and maybe a better job – when the child left the school. The Birmingham children who forsook the selling of Christmas novelties on street corners – and the income it provided – were given a treat: they were taken to see the skeleton of a whale at Curzon Hall.

Imagine that. Enjoy your stomach filled with Christmas goose? Or enjoy the sight of a dead mammal's skeleton? Tough choice.

Other children were on a half-time system that permitted them to work *and* go to school. The working kids arrived exhausted, underfed and shoeless to learn the names of the six wives of Henry VIII … who were neither undernourished nor shoeless. Or the date of Magna Carta … which granted supposed freedoms that the poor would never enjoy in the mills and the mines.

Holy Moses

Education is useless without the Bible. The Bible was America's basic text book in all fields. God's Word, contained in the Bible, has furnished all necessary rules to direct our conduct.

> Noah Webster (1748–1853), American writer

The Christian religion played an important part in the school day, from prayers and singing to learning catechism and analysing biblical texts. It may sound like an inappropriate use of childhood to us today, but even in Victorian times, it was criticised. Charles Dickens visited a ragged school at Field Lane – 'among the most miserable and neglected outcasts in London' – and used the experience to inform *A Christmas Carol* and *Oliver Twist*.

What did the Religious Education in the schools teach the miserable and neglected? That it simply taught them …

> *to look forward in a hymn (they sang it) to another life, which would correct the miseries and woes of this.*
>
> Charles Dickens, in a letter on ragged schooling in *The Daily News*

Understandably, the teachers were the most visible members of the system to blame. A teacher said:

I remember how, early in my career as a teacher, I had to avoid various missiles thrown at me by angry parents who would rather have the children running errands or washing up things in the home than wasting their time in school with such things as learning.

The school board inspectors, who had to enforce attendance, had to go around in pairs in some districts to protect one another from angry parents.

In some areas, school fees would be paid for the poorest families by the school board.

Compulsory education was a laudable idea, but the administrators had no idea *what* to teach the children, apart from religion, readin', writin', and 'rithmetic – a curriculum never known as 'The 4 Rs' for some reason.

It was usually rote learning and the old system of a single master/ mistress assisted by older children persisted from the grammar schools. Rote learning may not be the best way of preparing a child for the adult world.

Education is not filling a bucket but lighting a fire.

William Butler Yeats

The floors of the schoolrooms were often tiered so the children sitting at the back of the room were higher than those sitting at the front. All of the children had a clear view of the teacher and the blackboard. The teacher had a good view of them.

The windows in a Victorian classroom were high up so the pupils couldn't be distracted by a sight of the real world outside.

It must have been so *boring* that not all children could cope. They misbehaved, so 'punishment' had to be inflicted. Victorian punishments were every bit as sadistic as the mediaeval private and grammar schools had been. But there was a terrific amount of support from the Bible. If a poor parent dared to complain – they wouldn't – then they could be referred to the Bible ... which they probably couldn't read.

Chasten thy son while there is hope and let not thy soul spare for his crying.

King James Bible, Proverbs, XIX, 18

⇨ Boys were usually caned on their backsides and girls their bare legs or across their hands. The gentle Scots preferred a leather strap – the 'tawse'. It was for their own good, remember ...

Withhold not correction from the child; for if thou beatest him with a rod, thou shalt deliver his soul from hell.

King James Bible, Proverbs, XXIII, 13–14

⇨ A child (who needed to be saved from Hell) could be placed in a Punishment Basket, which was raised from the ground by ropes and pulleys and suspended from the ceiling.

Foolishness is bound in the heart of a child; but the rod of correction shall drive it from him.[4]

King James Bible, Proverbs, XXII, 15

⇨ Pinching, anywhere on the body, was a short-sharp-shock type of punishment and almost certainly not recorded in the class punishment book.

Judgements are prepared for scorners, and stripes for the backs of fools.

King James Bible, Proverbs, XIX, 29

⇨ Finger stocks were designed to stop children from fidgeting with their fingers. They comprised two small wooden plates, each with four holes in. The offending child would put one finger into each hole and the ribbons joining the two plates would be tied together behind the child's back, making it impossible for them to fiddle or twiddle.

A whip for a horse, a bridle for an ass, and a rod for a fool's back.

King James Bible, Proverbs, XXIX, 15

The Bible dominated the thinking in the schooling system. But as a clever man once said:

So far as I can remember, there is not one word in the Gospels in praise of intelligence.

Bertrand Russell (1872–1970), British philosopher

---

4. There are still teachers of a biblical inclination in Britain. In a 2008 poll, 22 per cent of secondary school teachers supported 'the right to use corporal punishment in extreme cases'. The number of pupils supporting the use of corporal punishment on teachers was not recorded. But surely, what's sauce for the goose …

Mental cruelty was all part of the teacher's armoury. Nothing changes. A slow learner could be made to wear a 'dunce's cap', an armband or a badge with the word 'dunce' written on it.

The Victorian schools were obliged to teach girls, of course. In the afternoons the girls and boys were segregated. The boys were taught woodworking and some schools also taught farming, shoemaking and gardening. The girls were taught how to cook meals, how to do embroidery, washing and ironing.

The legislators looked at the public schools of the past and threw in subjects like 'Geography' or 'History'. Not exciting history, of course, but suitable for rote learning.

The ragged schools for ragged children

Harsh as the 1870 Education Act schools were, there had been worse in the earlier days of the Empress Victoria's reign. Keeping street urchin children off the streets had been the job of the master of the town's ragged school.

Dickens described the ragged schools as for those less fortunate children.

They who are too ragged, wretched, filthy, and forlorn, to enter any other place: who could gain admission into no charity school, and who would be driven from any church door; are invited to come in here and find some people not depraved, willing to teach them something.

Charles Dickens, in a letter on ragged schooling in *The Daily News*

Sadly, there were people who WERE depraved and prepared to take on the unedifying job of apprehending then caring for and schooling urchins. Anyone with a university degree or teaching qualification need not apply.

Bedern Hall became a sausage factory, but the restless spirits of the dead children are still haunting the streets around the place. Walk down Bedern and hear playful laughter … or feel a small, cold hand take hold of yours.

The story of Mr Pimm may have been mythologised down the years, but the deprivation of pauper children in the ragged schools was real enough.

Charles Dickens said that the great and the good of Victorian England expended fortunes on new churches where God – not to mention the great and the good – could have their goodness and mercy praised. Could the Victorian philanthropists, perhaps, divert a little of that money to the ragged schools? It seemed not.

Did you know ...?

In York, the man appointed to organise the city's ragged school was Mr Pimm – less of a teacher, more of a child-catcher. His school stood at Bedern Hall and this sort of orphanage-cum-workhouse was officially known as the 'York Industrial Ragged School'.

Mr Pimm was paid handsomely to round up local waifs and strays and put them to work. He kept a register of the children who worked there and was paid for each child. The money was to be used for food and clothing for the children, but without official school inspectors,[5] there were no checks and balances on how he spent the money ... in his case, minimal expense on the waifs and maximum in his pocket.

Without the modicum of food and clothing, many of the children died through cold or starvation.

Funerals were another expense he could do without. He'd have buried them in the garden of Bedern Hall but in a harsh winter the earth was too hard to dig. He stuffed them in a cupboard till there was a thaw. And a funeral would have meant declaring the child dead and off the register. By disposing of the bodies himself, he could keep the child on the register and still claim the council's money.

This soon became a common practice to him, and he'd keep those bodies in his cupboard until he had enough to bury them in one go.

As months passed, Mr Pimm started hearing otherworldly children's voices and was sure the spirits of the children had returned to haunt him. One night, he took to strong drink and went mad, mutilating the children he had still in his care with a knife.

He was found the next morning snivelling amongst the little bodies and was locked away in an asylum for the remainder of his life.

It consisted at that time of either two or three miserable rooms, upstairs in a miserable house. In the best of these, the pupils in the female school were being taught to read and write. The appearance of this room was sad and melancholy, of course – how could it be otherwise! – but, on the whole, encouraging.

Charles Dickens, in a letter on ragged schooling in *The Daily News*

---

5. Or Ofstapo, as teachers call them today.

The boys in an adjacent room had a very different experience

The close, low chamber at the back, in which the boys were crowded, was so foul and stifling as to be, at first, almost insupportable. Huddled together on a bench about the room, and shown out by some flaring candles stuck against the walls, were a crowd of boys.

It wasn't simply the classroom. It was the instruction.

Its moral aspect was so far worse than its physical, that this was soon forgotten. They varied from mere infants to young men; sellers of fruit, herbs, lucifer-matches, flints; sleepers under the dry arches of bridges; young thieves and beggars – with nothing natural to youth about them: with nothing frank, ingenuous, or pleasant in their faces; low-browed, vicious, cunning, wicked; abandoned of all help but this; speeding downward to destruction; and UNUTTERABLY IGNORANT.[6]

The aim of the ragged schools was to teach the unfortunates to accept their place in God's grand scheme of things. Their Earthly home was not a happy place. Dickens's plea to the rich to pay for schooling for the underclasses was a forlorn hope. Monarchs like Henry VIII were praised for establishing grammar schools, but they were never intended for the sons of the peasantry. As for girls … their education was not even thought of enough to be unthinkable.

> *I don't like Mondays. This livens up the day.*
> Brenda Spencer, who in 1979, at 16 years old,
> killed two adults, wounded eight children
> and one police officer at a school

---

6. Maybe read that passage again? The writing style of Charles Dickens was criticised by contemporary George Eliot as 'having no proficiency in drawing "psychological character"'. But absorb this passage and you're more inclined to agree with Thackeray, who read *Dombey and Son*, burst into Dickens's office and exclaimed: 'There's no writing against such power as this – one has no chance.'

Epilogue

Suffrage, noun. Expression of opinion by means of a ballot. The right of suffrage (which is held to be both a privilege and a duty) means, as commonly interpreted, the right to vote for the man of another man's choice and is highly prized.

Ambrose Bierce (1842–1914), American journalist

A little girl once asked me, 'If you could live at any time in history, which would you choose?' This wise but elderly writer answered (wisely), 'The age in which I grew up. The 1950s.'

The little girl frowned as she tried to place my golden age. 'Was that the Middle Ages?' she asked.

'No, it wasn't,' I replied … as I signed her book '*Geoffrey Chaucer*'.

The true heroes of history are not the conquering kings, the winning warriors or the empire builders. They are Mr and Ms Peasant. Their names may be mostly forgotten, perhaps recorded (if at all) in some dust-laden parish register. Their actions are largely unremembered unless they performed some deed that the literate thought worth recording. An underclass man like Jack Crawford, for example.

The tale of two heroes

How do chroniclers of history decide who is worth remembering? Look at two similar cases of heroic sailors in the Napoleonic Wars:

1. Jack Crawford

Jack was born in 1775 in the east end of Sunderland. In 1797, when Jack was aged 22, he was press-ganged into serving on board *The Venerable*, the leading ship of Admiral Duncan's fleet. This was a very dangerous year for England. The French, led by Napoleon, were winning all the battles on land.

The French had forced the navies of Holland and Spain to join them in the war. There were now three strong navies lined up to fight against Britain. If they joined up in the open seas, they would smash the British navy and invade.

In 1797, Admiral Duncan had the task of watching the Dutch fleet and stopping them from leaving their harbour. When the Dutch fleet came out of the harbour, the Battle of Camperdown followed. A shell broke the top part of *The Venerable*'s mast and the Admiral's flag fell to the deck. The Admiral's flag going down was a sign to the rest of the fleet to cease fire and sail away.

Admiral Duncan called: 'Is there any man who will climb up the remains of the mast and fix the flag back on?'

Jack Crawford replied: 'I'll do it, sir.'

Shells were flying everywhere, and the air was thick with bullets. While Jack was nailing the flag, a splinter from a shot struck the mast and went through his cheek. But thanks to Jack Crawford, the flag and the British fleet triumphed, the battle was won and (perhaps) Britain was saved from a French invasion.

After the battle, Jack had to be fed through a straw for six weeks, because of his wounds.

After the peace, Jack returned to Sunderland. He had to live with the heavy weight of the title 'National hero'.

The people of Sunderland were proud of their local hero and to show their love of him he was presented with a large silver medal, engraved:

The town of Sunderland to Jack Crawford, for gallant services, the 11th October 1797.

In 1831, a ship brought the deadly disease cholera to Sunderland. One of the first to die was Jack Crawford. The disease did what French shells and bullets couldn't and finished him off.

He was buried in an unmarked grave.

2. The Most Noble Lord Horatio Nelson, Viscount and Baron Nelson, of the Nile and of Burnham Thorpe in the County of Norfolk, Baron Nelson of the Nile and of Hillborough in the said County, Knight of the Most Honourable Order of the Bath, Vice Admiral of the White Squadron of the Fleet, Commander in Chief of his Majesty's Ships and Vessels in the Mediterranean, Duke of Bronte in Sicily, Knight Grand Cross of the Sicilian Order of St Ferdinand and of Merit, Member of the Ottoman Order of the Crescent, Knight Grand Commander of the Order of St. Joachim[1]

Eight years after the Battle of Camperdown, the British won the Battle of Trafalgar. Admiral Lord Nelson didn't nail any flags to the mast and was

---

1. Titles inscribed on his coffin ... either in very small writing or on a very large coffin.

really an unsavoury character.[2] He foolishly paraded himself on the deck of his ship, in all his glittering awards, and was duly shot by an enemy sniper … leaving the British fleet exposed without its commander.

Jack Crawford was buried in a pauper's grave. Later he was honoured with a small statue that stands in a park in Sunderland.

Admiral Lord Nelson was given a state funeral: George III cried for him and the Prince of Wales led the four-hour funeral service attended by thirty-two admirals, over a hundred captains, and an escort of 10,000 soldiers. He was buried in St Paul's Cathedral. Innumerable monuments and memorials were constructed across the country, and abroad – including a mighty column in the centre of London.[3] Nelson comfortably topped a poll of the greatest military hero in 800 years of British military history.

Nelson was a lord and a brave man. Jack Crawford was a peasant and an equally brave man.

Lords are remembered. Peasants are forgotten. Two nations.

All animals are equal, but some animals are more equal than others.

George Orwell, in *Animal Farm*

Next time someone asks me to name Britain's greatest hero, I shall answer, 'Mr and Ms Peasant'.

The majority will go on answering 'Lord Nelson' – probably not the 99-word coffin-plaque version of his name – rather than 'Jack Crawford'.

It's enough to make a peasant revolt.

END

---

2. To give but one example, Nelson was a friend of slave traders and wrote, 'While I have a tongue, I will launch my voice against the damnable and cursed doctrine of Wilberforce (the abolitionist) and his hypocritical allies.'

3. Nelson's Column is visited by more tourists than Crawford's column. It is also visited by more pigeons.

Index

Index

Index

169

Index